GRIEF *and* GLORY *in* LAMENTATIONS

Seeking Hope and Healing for the Grieving Heart

Dr. Danny Emory

Grief and Glory in Lamentations

All passages of Scripture are from the New King James Version unless otherwise specified.

ISBN 978-1-940645-90-2

Greenville, South Carolina

Published in the United States of America

Dedication

This writing is dedicated to those who have felt the grief of loss and separation of someone who was deeply loved.

Table of Contents

Foreword

Grief, sorrow, and sadness are a part of life. In *Grief and Glory in Lamentations,* Dr. Danny Emory explains that grief is simply the love we no longer can convey or extend to the person or object lost.

Dr. Emory draws on over 40 years of ministry and over 65 years of life experience to present a thorough and precise understanding of this somewhat neglected book. He offers a scholarly yet tremendously practical exposition of the weeping prophet's lamentations. Writing from a pastor's heart, his goal is to offer hope and encouragement to those walking through the Valley of Baca (weeping and sorrow). He is very personal and transparent as he details many of his own trials and sorrows and explains how God has used them to draw him closer to Himself.

First Peter 5:6-7 says, "Humble yourselves therefore under the mighty hand of God, that He may exalt you in due time, casting all your care upon Him, for He cares for you." Although the journey through the grief process can be long, arduous, and painful, Dr. Emory describes that when navigated patiently and properly, it can deepen our walk with our Savior and bring Him glory as well.

This book will be a valuable resource, not only for pastors and theologians, but for everyone — because each of us eventually will travel the road of sorrow just as Job, Jeremiah, and even Jesus did centuries ago.

Rev. Joe Seay
Campobello, S.C.

Preface

The Book of Lamentations is God's handbook on grief. The writer, Jeremiah, is a mighty spokesman for God, and he is also very much human. He surveys his beloved city, Jerusalem, and sees the destruction within it and the loss among the people. He then expresses his grief to his readers. Within these verses there is both grief and glory as Jeremiah reveals his soul. There are moments when the writer takes you to the depth of sorrow for the people who have lost so much of their possessions and culture. There are other moments when Jeremiah writes words that lift your soul to heavenly heights. Therefore, through each verse, the reader is given a front-row seat to the scenes of both grief and glory.

This writing is not intended to cover every aspect of grief from the standpoint of a professional therapist. I lay no claim to have explored every aspect of the subject of grief. This writing comes from the pen of a pastor who has not lived in the safe zone of an ivory tower, but who has been with many who have walked through the valley of grief and who also have experienced grief in personal ways.

Lamentations is a very "real life" book. It is not for the faint of heart, but neither is grief. This book pulsates with human emotions that serve as mirrors to our own souls. Jeremiah is not afraid to ask the questions that we quietly ask to ourselves. There are times when he receives no answer, yet he continues his walk with God in faith. There are many times when we grieve and there seems to be no answer for our loss. We should follow the example of Jeremiah and trust God's promises rather than seeking answers.

In this preface I want to give the reader the definition of grief as it is referred to in this writing. Grief is the result of a loss. It is the emotional backlash of something taken from you that you loved very deeply.

Jamie Anderson says: "Grief, I've learned, is really just love. It's all the love you want to give but cannot. All that unspent love gathers up in the corners of your eyes, the lump in your throat, and in that hollow part of your chest. Grief is just love with no place to go."[1]

That love which is taken from your presence is not taken from your heart. It is the loss that causes us to grieve. This loss may be in the form of the death of a spouse, child or close friend. It may be the loss of a job, a pet, or a relationship that is cooled by separation or that never materialized. The grief from loss is as varied as the personalities that grieve.

My desire for this writing is that as you read you will find something that gives you hope. My greatest passion is for you to find hope in *Someone* whose name is Jesus Christ. He will never stop loving you regardless of all your failures. He will never leave you as an orphan to make the trip of grief by yourself. He can be depended on! He is truth! He is the only source of hope we have in this hurting world. If you find that people, things, and social positions leave you hopeless, get your focus on Jesus because He is life, light, and love, and He will never fail to satisfy your deepest needs.

"The reality is that you will grieve forever. You will not 'get over' the loss of a loved one; you will learn to live with it. You will heal and rebuild yourself around the loss you have suffered. You will be whole again, but you will never be the same. Nor should you be the same nor would you want to," Elisabeth Kübler-Ross and David Kesseer state.[2]

I have no idea how God will use this writing. My desire is that those who read it will find some encouragement, hope and motivation to push through the grief and allow God to use it to help someone else (2 Corinthians 1:4-7).

May God bless the eyes that look upon these pages.

— Dr. Danny Emory

Notes

1. https://www.goodreads.com/author/quotes/3395454.Jamie_Anderson.

2. Elisabeth Kübler-Ross and David Kesseer, *On Grief and Grieving*, (New York: Scribner, 2005), 230.

Acknowledgments

Thanks to my wife, Barbara, whose encouragement kept me motivated to continue to write. I am grateful to my daughters, Danielle Wheeler, Diana Williams and Dedra Sain. Their anguish of losing a child helped me understand the pain of losing a child.

I would be in error if I did not recognize those who read and corrected the many mistakes of a first-time writer. Dawn Seay and Morgan Buchanan were helpful in proofreading the material. I owe a great deal of gratitude to Troy Houser for the final reading and corrections of the manuscript. His insight and input proved to be immensely valuable.

Last but not least, I acknowledge Katherine Houser who typed this writing. She worked tirelessly to "make me look good" on paper.

I appreciate The Baptist Courier for publishing my writing. The publishing department has allowed me this wonderful opportunity to have this book printed.

Most of all, I thank Jesus Christ for allowing me to grow through the grief that comes as a result of a loss. Jesus did not allow me to go through my experience without a purpose. He brought me through the grief to see the glory of His person and power to heal. His grace is sufficient.

GRIEF *and* GLORY *in* LAMENTATIONS

Seeking Hope and Healing for the Grieving Heart

Introduction

The writings before you are not the products of a scholar. Although much research is invested upon both subjects of grief and Lamentations, I do not write from a tower of scholarship. Neither is this work an in-depth commentary on the Book of Lamentations. Certainly, I will attempt to explain the writings of Lamentations; however, I have chosen not to take the scholarly route. Instead, I have intentionally chosen to show the brilliance of God's word in Lamentations in a simple way. These are the writings of a simple pastor/teacher who has experienced grief on many occasions and has attempted to help others walk through the process of grief.

The purpose of my writing is to gain an understanding of grief as it is expressed through the Book of Lamentations. The nation of Judah is grieving because of the destruction of the nation and deportation of her people. This is God's judgment against the people's rebellion toward Him. The capitol city of Judah is Jerusalem. Jerusalem serves as an illustration of a nation in grief because they have lost their families, homes, leaders, city and country. The people of Jerusalem are expressing their grief to God in hopes of His healing.

My hope and prayer is that God will use this simple study to help many people who have been deeply hurt by the loss of someone or something they loved and held very close. I trust that through the truth of God's word as it is applied to your injured spirit, you will find he. and maturity that will help you move through the pain.

Summary of Lamentations

Again, let me remind the reader that my purpose in this writing is not to dive into the depths of this sacred yet sad book. I desire only to communicate truth and marry that truth to the grieving human heart. With that thought, let's seek to know the author of the Book of Lamentations.

The first task is to discover who the author of Lamentations is. I would like to tell you with great authority who the writer is, but I cannot with certainty because no name is attached to the writing. For centuries the prophet Jeremiah has been considered to be the author. Although his authorship has been challenged, I believe that traditional wisdom is valuable and useable for this study. Therefore, I do believe that the Book of Lamentations was written by Jeremiah and that he was under the inspiration of the Holy Spirit.

Here are a few of the reasons I choose to believe Jeremiah to be the author of Lamentations:

Number 1: Lamentations was written by someone who was on the scene when Jerusalem fell to the Babylonian army. He writes from the "front row" of all that took place as the people suffered and the walls fell down around the city.

Number 2: The earliest Greek translation of the Hebrew Old Testament helps us arrive at this viewpoint. The Septuagint says, "And it came to pass, after Israel was taken captive and Jerusalem laid waste, that Jeremiah sat weeping and lamented with this lamentation over Jerusalem." Second Chronicles 35:25 offers support with these words:

And Jeremiah lamented for Josiah: and all the singing men and all the singing women spake of Josiah in their lamentations to this day, and made them an ordinance in Israel: and, behold, they are written in the lamentations (KJV).

I acknowledge that Josiah's name is not found in Lamentations. There are many differences as well as similarities between the style of the writer of Lamentations and Jeremiah's prophetic writings. However, there is not enough material for one to deny Jeremiah as the author of Lamentations.

Number 3: The word "Jeremiad," according to Merriam Webster, means a "prolonged lamentation of complaint." Because the prophet had a "front-row seat" to the destruction of his beloved city, he experienced the bitter pain of loss and expressed his grief with tears (Jeremiah 14:17, 9:1; Lamentations 3:1).

Lamentations is a book that does connect with the Book of Jeremiah, but it is not Jeremiah part two. Lamentations is a revelation of the inner soul of Jeremiah. Therein, we observe his response to what he sees and feels as he witnesses the fall of Jerusalem as a result of the wrath of God upon the people. Concerning questions about the authorship of Lamentations, the King James Version titles the book, "The Lamentations of Jeremiah." The Nelson Study Bible of the New King James Version in its "plaintive outcry" reveals the broken heart of the prophet Jeremiah, and for most biblical scholars Jeremiah is the writer of Lamentations. The Nelson Study Bible goes on to state that "Jeremiah expresses his grief" over the national tragedy that was unfolding before his eyes.

My final statement concerning the authorship of Lamentations is simple and honest. It really does not matter who the author is. The truth is, Lamentations is not the journal of an individual who suffers and grieves from a personal loss. The book is the recording of a nation which suffers grief and loss. However, the book also reveals that by turning to God, they found a way out of darkness into light, out of despair into hope, and out of doubt into greater faith.

The time and style of Lamentations can be identified with certainty. The writing is after the fall of Jerusalem in 587 or 586 B.C. The construction of the book is not foreign to biblical writing, but it is quite unique because it sends a comforting message to the reader. The book is a collection of five poems/songs that would be used in funerals or special feast times in Judah.

These poems/songs are written in the form of the acrostic style. Chapters 1, 2 and 4 each have twenty-two verses. There are twenty-two letters in the Hebrew alphabet. Each verse begins in Chapters 1, 2 and 4 in successive order with one of the twenty-two letters of the Hebrew alphabet. Chapter 3 has sixty-six verses — three times the number of the other four chapters. Chapter 3 runs in triplet form. For example, the first three verses begin with the first letter of the alphabet, each of the next three verses begin with the second letter of the alphabet, and that pattern continues to the end of the sixty-six verses with the entire twenty-two letters of the alphabet. Chapter 5 does not have the acrostic form of writing, but the number of verses is twenty-two, which corresponds to the number of the Hebrew alphabet.[1] Chapters 1, 2 and 4 are dirges (a lament for the dead said at a funeral). Chapter 3 is a personal lament that concludes with a prayer. Chapter 5 is also a prayer.

The use of the acrostic style of writing begs the question: Why did the author write in this style? Without a doubt there is a "method to his madness." In the English, it can be said that the writer covers his story line from A to Z and all that is between. This is a message of fulfillment and completion. The writer completely reveals this story of inner pain and remorse. He has poured out his soul in full fashion for the reader to see. He has held back no feeling. He has fully and completely covered everything in his confession and repentance to God. He has left "no stone unturned" in his sad story. In response, God gives the reader a fulfillment of His mercy, love, and compassion during the devastation of the land.

For his full and complete story, we are grateful. On a personal basis, this book has great value. One finds it easy to identify with Jeremiah in the human experience of loss. God gives us words of hope, encouragement, and a call to refocus on Him through Jeremiah's penmanship. Our voice is heard in this book. We learn the value of hope and mercy in God. The Lamentations help us better understand the workings of God in the midst of human suffering and gives hope that lives can be rebuilt after a devastating loss.

From a theological viewpoint, Lamentations is of great worth. Within these verses, there is the honest expression of a suffering soul. The writer asks in public the same questions that the believer asks privately, such as, "God, should you treat your own people this way?" For example, he asks this question in Chapter 2: "Should the women eat their offspring, the children they have cuddled?" (2:20).

In the vernacular of today, the question could be phrased, "God, don't you care that your people suffer?" Chapter 3, verse 36 says, "Or subvert man in his cause — the Lord does not approve."

In other words, the searching question to God is, "God, are you not involved with the injustices in our world?" Questions from Chapter 5, verse 22 state: "Unless you have utterly rejected us, and are very angry with us."

Often these questions are hurled at God. To grieve is human, and to question is also human. Personally, I think God is great and loving enough to withstand our questions.

From the theological view in Lamentations, one can see the holiness of God as He chastises His people. His love for people is expressed as He never gives up on them and pursues them that they might return to Him. His grace toward them is revealed in His patience for them.

God's judgment toward His very own people is proof that He desires them to be holy and committed only unto Him. There is much here to observe concerning the nature of God.

Prayer and petitioning to God are well noted in Lamentations. Jeremiah pleads to God to heal the people and not forsake them. This shows us not only the faith of Jeremiah in God, but it also shows God's attention to man's need. We see the compassion that God has as He helps those who hurt from grief. God helps the broken. He favors those who call out to Him. Throughout this book, the writer expresses his feelings of isolation, failure, and sadness, yet he always finds reason to rely upon the trustworthiness of God in prayer.

There is tremendous value to the grieving heart of a child of God. Lamentations does not offer a customized set of answers to the questions of life. Instead, the book points us to the faithfulness of God.

These verses serve as a salve to the soul of anyone who has a broken heart. Throughout the reading of these five poems/songs, you and I discover they are in rhythm with the grief-stricken person. There are highs and lows of feelings. There is the loss of hope and the discovery of a new hope in the heart of a grief-stricken person.

One would expect to discover in these five short chapters a theme that starts with a note of desperation and despair and builds as a musical crescendo that ends with hopeful jubilation in the last chapter. This is not the case in Lamentations, as it is in the Book of Ruth, Job, or Revelation. The reason for this is that each chapter builds to its own peak of hopefulness in God. Robert Laurin makes an excellent point when he says:

> There is another facet to this. Although the book expects the end of exile (4:22), longs for political restoration (5:21), and waits for personal vengeance (1:21-22, 4:21-22), yet it is content to leave the future in the hands of Yahweh. Since His present actions are mysterious, so His future actions will be as well. This is a vital contribution of the Book of Lamentations. It sets no dates, prescribes no patterns. It simply says that the future is bright with promise for those who have overcome doubt in trustful reliance upon the Lord.[2]

The beginning of hope is found in the heart of faith for those who trust in an all wise, perfect, sovereign God. He knows us better than we know ourselves. We can trust Him with the pain. When we allow God to do His work, we will soon discover that not only will God give us a new hope, He will give us a new us. With a new mindset comes a new appreciation for the perfect character of God. At the end of a broken, grieving heart is a wonderful light of the God Who has loved us and led us through the grief process. When we pass through the pain, we might say as Jeremiah did in Chapter 3, verse 23: "They are new every morning; great is Your faithfulness."

NOTES

1. J. Sidlow Baxter, *Explore the Book,* (Grand Rapids: Zondervan Publishing House), 281.

2. Robert B. Laurin, *The Broadman Commentary, Vol. 6,* (Nashville: Broadman Press, 1971), 101.

Chapter 1
Prophet of Grief

My daddy succumbed to a horrible disease in 2003. For six difficult years he was on dialysis. He was constantly in and out of the hospital for various infections and problems that were associated with his disease. I stood by helplessly and watched a very strong man become weaker and frailer with each passing day. I recognized the power of his illness and knew that his illness would ultimately win the victory over him. I accepted that in time he would leave my mother, sister, five grandchildren and me. He lived five-and-one-half years longer than the doctors first predicted. However, death overcame him.

As a pastor, I have seen this scenario play out many times in the lives of people. But this time it was different. This time it was my daddy, part of me, part of my family. This was too close to my heart. To have a close relative or friend taken from you by death is never easy, even when you have time to prepare yourself. I thought that I had come to a level of acceptance of his impending death. I was wrong.

Countless times I have stood before a grieving family. I reminded them of Bible verses that were laced with the promises of God that He would never leave us, always love us, and that His peace would guard our hearts in troubled times. I believed that truth with all my heart, but I said all those things with faith for I never had experienced a parent's passing. Now was the time when I had to put into practice what I had said to hurting people for thirty years. After all, people were watching me to see how I would act in times of bereavement. I tried to be strong and display an example to others of how a Christian should respond to the death of my father. Looking back, I put too much on my heart that no one expected but me. No one ever told me that I had to be strong, or that I had to be an example to others. This was self-imposed and so unnecessary. Although I knew some of the ways to help people at funeral services, I never knew the depth of their inner pain. Neither did I understand the longevity of their bereavement. I was about to be educated in the classroom of grief.

In fact, I did not know how to grieve in a productive and Christ-honoring way. Neither did I have time to grieve. In two weeks I was busy attending to a family experiencing the death of their loved one. On my day off, I was very busy attending to the closing of my dad's affairs. I was in the church every Sunday, trying to present my best ministry performance to the church family. The truth is, I had a delayed grief response about two years after my dad's passing, and then I had to be told by a trained counselor that I was experiencing clinical depression as a result of a loss. I never grieved as I should have, and the results were not good.

Much has transpired in my life since December 3, 2003, when my daddy died. I still miss him. I wish I could seek his wisdom to answer some questions. Occasionally, I sit at his grave and think. But he is gone. I had to learn to grieve my loss. I grew through the loss of my dad as well as four other deeply personal losses. I believe that I learned some things that I can use to help others grieve. As stated earlier, this is the purpose for my writing. I seek to help those who grieve the losses of life to pass through the pain in such a way that Christ is honored.

I have chosen to study a book of the Bible that I have never studied in depth. I have preached a section of the Book of Lamentations, but I had never examined it as closely as I have recently. Walter C. Kaiser calls this book the "orphan book" of the Bible.[1] This is a fitting description because it is seldom studied and is given little attention from the pulpits of our churches. This is a sad truth for within these five chapters is the record of a nation that has lost her people, properties, and position in the world. The people of Jerusalem are in deep despair and national grief. My prayer is that God will provide some spiritual truths as to how grief is unpackaged in our lives and how we grieve and recover from the harshness of a great loss.

The first chapter begins with the word "how" in the King James Version. Chapters 2 and 4 begin with the same word. In fact, "how" is the Hebrew title of the Book of Lamentations. It is translated as "Ah, how!" Another Hebrew word means "elegies" or lamentations.[2] The word "how" expresses exclamation. The word "how" is used to introduce funeral dirges (Jeremiah 48:17). The people expressed astonishment that God would allow these sufferings to come to them. They were the ones God declared to be His people and the ones He loved so deeply. How could He allow such suffering to those He claimed to love so deeply?

The Reality of the Pain

Chapter 1 begins by presenting a picture of deep despair and hopelessness. However, eventually the wonderful light of God's character shines through the darkness. This chapter reveals the mourning of the people over the loss of their nation, Judah, and the loss of the capital city, Jerusalem. This is a portrait of a people gripped by national grief.

The concern of these mourners is twofold: (1) What is the reason for the heavy losses of the people? (2) What did the losses consist of? The reason for their loss is not hard to discover. The judgment of Holy God fell upon the people because they participated in grievous sins against God (1:5-8). The scar of sin not only marked the common people of Judah, but also the leadership of both the political and religious systems.

Second Kings 21:1-9, 16 gives us a list of their sins. King Manasseh constructed altars for Baal. He himself bowed to worship the powers of the heavens. He led the people of Judah to reject God while encouraging them to practice sorcery and witchcraft, and to consult with mediums and psychics. As a result, the anger of God was aroused against them. Second Kings 24, verses 3 and 4 teach us that these disasters came to Judah because of the many sins of Manasseh (NLT). A second group of Scriptures that lists the sins the people did against God is found in 2 Chronicles 33:1-10, 33:22-23, and 36:11-16.

Sinful actions against God never pay profitable dividends. Sin pays in deficits. This truth is for us today as well as it was for Judah. Sin is a lose-lose proposition. The people had become a reproach to God and would certainly pay for their rebellion. Judah enjoyed the immorality and never considered the payment for their rebellion. Judah never thought that God would punish them for they were His covenant people. However, God responded in judgment. God's righteous anger rose to a boiling point and spilled over in the invasion of the Babylonian army, who destroyed the country and deported many people to Babylonia. No one escapes the judgment of Holy God.

What are some of the things the nation of Judah lost and grieved over? Verses 1-4 speak of their loss of prominence. Verses 5-8 speak of their loss of position. And verses 9-17 speak of their loss of power. All of these losses left the people with a sense of isolation, emptiness and misery. Such are the payments of sin against God.

First, they lost their prominence. This is revealed in verses 1-4. Perhaps the loss of prominence is best understood by way of contrast between what they had and what they lost. Verse 1 speaks of a time when Jerusalem was full of people who were involved with the lucrative business of buying and selling merchandise. Multitudes would make their journey to Jerusalem to offer sacrifices and worship to God. God blessed them with a city of wonderful points of interest for travelers from all over the known world. After God's judgment, the contrast is evident. The throngs of people are gone. The city is deserted. Jerusalem was once a "princess" among the nations. The lady of prominence now sits as a lonely weeping widow. At one time she was a great ruler in the world, but now she is reduced to the standing of a simple slave.

Verse 2 describes Jerusalem as previously having "many lovers" or many allegiances with friendly nations. She forsook her dependence on God for these lovers only to discover they were not trustworthy. She believed that she could depend on her "lovers" during attacks from her foes. Now those friends have been replaced by enemies. As a result, Jerusalem feels the loss of her friends. She cries all night for the hurt and betrayal from those she trusted. Nothing pierces the heart of a lover like the act of betrayal. She certainly felt the pain of being forsaken. One can somewhat understand her pain because it is revealed in verse 2 when Jerusalem says, "She weeps bitterly in the night, her tears are on her cheeks; among all her lovers she has none to comfort her. ... They have become her enemies." This is a recurring phrase used by the writer. He employs this phrase five times in verses 2, 9, 15, 17 and 21. In the phrase she expresses her feeling of forsakenness, loneliness, isolation, and the agony of trusting in unreliable associates.

Judah feels the loss of respect from other nations. She thinks she is being chased by her enemies. She has run to the point of exhaustion and now has no more places to run. You might say that the loss of prominence has placed her in an unending circle, never gaining a distance from her enemies (verse 3).

Verse 4 is very descriptive. At one time Jerusalem was a place that bustled with people who attended the celebration of various festivals. Now the people no longer come to this depressed city. The roads once filled with travelers are empty and easy to travel because no one comes to the city. The city gates where businessmen and leaders met to do business are now vacant. The temple that once was the pride of Jerusalem is destroyed, and the priests are jobless. The young ladies who hoped to marry sit and cry because their chances of marriage and having a family are few. There is a heavy, dark pall draped over the city to remind them of the death of the city. Jerusalem had lost her prominence among other nations in her region.

Judah and her capital city, Jerusalem, not only lost their prominent standing among other nations, but they also suffered the loss of the position of greatness among other nations (verses 5-13). Her sinful rejection of God's demands for the people resulted in a very costly end for them. This should prove to both a nation and an individual that when we flaunt the law of God, we will suffer the consequences of our choice.

At one time Judah was the master, but now she becomes the slave (verse 5). Her children are now the slaves of her enemies. Verse 6 features her loss of position in picturesque language. It describes the beauty of Jerusalem being stripped away. She is only a shell of her former glory. The government officials leave the ruined city in haste as a deer that is frightened by a hunter. These leaders show no compassion for those who are left behind and are too weak to flee. To add more humiliation to Jerusalem's hurt, her enemies ridicule and laugh as the once great city falls to the earth. There is no one to help her. She lives in the remembrance of her days of greatness and reflects upon her present misery (verse 7). Jerusalem previously was as a beautiful lady of charm and honor. Now she has lost her position of strength, and others are aware of this. She is reduced to the rank of a woman who is humiliated, defiled and rejected by her neighbors. She has lost her reputation and now hides her shameful face. She lies in the gutter of life and her "lovers" mock her. She is a living example of how one's sin can reduce them to a state of barrenness.

Her many resources were taken away by the Babylonian plunderers as they advanced themselves from Judah's wealth. Judah was left as a wanton beggar. However, sad as that is, it is not the greatest humiliation of the city. The temple, a place of sacredness to the people was invaded by the pagan Babylonian army. The insult was harsh, and the loss was very great in the minds of the people. Spiritual affliction led to physical starvation (verse 11). The Babylonian army was successful in maintaining an eighteen-month siege around Jerusalem. As a result, the crops that were in the field were left for the soldiers to eat or destroy. The barrier around the city prevented the farmers from planting their crops. Devastating starvation set upon the people. The starvation was so great that parents would often sell their children into slavery in order to purchase food. An even worse option was to resort to cannibalism so they could survive the siege. Certainly, the children were treasures the parents did not want to surrender. Second Kings 6:25-29, Jeremiah 37:21, 38:9, 52:6 and Lamentations 2:20-22 serve as references to this horrible experience of loss for the people.

Within these many losses, Judah also experienced the loss of power among other nations (verses 12-19). In this section of Lamentations, the author brilliantly describes the national loss of power. According to verse 12, the Lord was given credit for their loss of power in the form of fire. He had erupted like a volcano with fierce anger toward His people that burnt the inhabitants of the city down in their bones. The mighty army of Babylonia is credited with the destruction; however, they were only a tool in God's hands to bring judgment upon Judah. God is not limited when He chooses to send judgment upon a nation or a person. Here, God used pagans to punish His chosen people. The people of

Judah had sprung God's trap of judgment, and no one was able to escape. Sickness and starvation were the results of judgment upon the people. God is described as weaving their sins into heavy ropes that tied them to a yoke of slavery. The people felt the weight of their sins on their necks as a beast of burden carries a yoke. The weight of their sin overcame their strength and left them powerless in the hands of their tormentors (verse 14). Jeremiah employs a picture of Jerusalem being crushed like grapes in a winepress. The figure of the winepress is one of God's wrath (Isaiah 63:3; Revelation 14:19, 19:15).[3] The people felt rejected for God no longer served as their shield of protection. In fact, He proclaimed their defeat. The army of Babylonia crushed Jerusalem's army like grapes in a winepress.

Jerusalem is like an invalid upon a sick bed. She reaches out to anyone who might be willing to help, but no one offers. The city cries for someone to give comfort, yet no one seems to care. God has ordained her defeat and destruction. She is to be discarded as a rag of a menstruating woman. This is graphic in detail but descriptive as to their loss of power because of sin towards God.

Unrepentant, stubborn, prideful people pay a heavy price for spurning the call of God. Their losses are costly and remind us that there is no escape from the judgment of God when sin rules in our lives. The losses of prominence, position, and power among the neighboring peoples of Judah were high penalties to pay for their rebellion toward God.

No reasonable student of Lamentations will fail to observe how much the people of Judah lost as a result of their disobedience toward God. Their losses were many and great. Their agony over the destruction of the city of Jerusalem, the deportation of many of the people, and the death of so many children and young men who had great promise in life was more than they could bear. Losses in life always hurt our hearts. Even the slightest loss for some is enough to turn their emotions into a period of grief. Sometimes in life's journey the losses people encounter add up to be many, and if the grieving person does not deal with each loss in a healthy way, the next loss could be as a rushing river that breaks an emotional dam in his life. It is important that we respond in a healthy way to our losses. The question before us is, how should we respond to our loss? Let us examine how the people of Judah responded in their losses, and that may help equip us to deal properly with ours.

The Responses of the People (18-22)

The proper response is extremely important for anyone who grieves after a loss. The people of Judah made a proper response as they made confession to God. It was to God that the people made a very courageous confession. They admitted that God is righteous.

They confessed that God was right in what He did. Personally, I have found such enormous relief in my soul when I simply admit this truth concerning our sovereign God. He is always right and never wrong in what He allows me to experience in the losses of my life. He is perfect and just in all of His ways toward me. There are many times that I have not been able to clear away the dust from the experience and see God as right in His ways. However, His ways are not our ways. His thoughts are higher than mine (Isaiah 55:9). As I experience grief, I am not able to see His entire plan for me. It is only when I look back upon my journey with Him that I can see the larger picture and admit, yes, He is right in all of His ways with me. At the time I may not like what He has allowed to come into my life, but God does not have to ask my permission to do what His perfect and holy character allows. Nor does He give me the entire blueprint of the future development of my life. He simply works in me from the standpoint of His righteousness.

Admitting that God is right in what He did to the people of Judah was the correct starting place for them and for us as well. It shows our humility and submission to Him. We recognize His superiority over us and our brokenness to Him. God runs to give comfort to those who are humble before Him. In Chapter 1, the people of Jerusalem were on the correct path when they decided to return to God.

The second confession they made is found in verse 18 as well. They admitted they had rebelled against His commandments (18b). Their admission is twofold: God is right and they are wrong. They deserve the losses of their people and properties because of their rebellion against Him. The consequences of Judah's rebellion were harsh but just, because God is just.

The residents of Jerusalem confessed God as righteous. They attempted to reach out to others for sympathy only to find no solace from anyone. There are times when God isolates us only unto Himself, so we find our hope in Him alone. No one else gives that comfort to us or cries with us. God is taking away all the people who prop us up in life, so we run only to Him for instruction and help. When we are alone with God, He does His work in us to develop and conform us into the likeness of Christ. He cannot fully do that work if we are focusing on others and depending on their assistance. This is not to say we should totally isolate ourselves from others. People need people. However, there are times in our life when God wants us only to Himself.

Let's observe three episodes in the life of biblical characters that illustrate this truth. My mind recalls Joseph, who was falsely accused and placed into prison for a crime he did not commit. God could have allowed Joseph to go to court and prove himself innocent, but God had a better plan for him. God allowed Joseph to go to prison for several years. All along, God developed him and prepared him to be in the position to save the Hebrew people from starvation. Without a doubt, God put Joseph in a place of isolation so He could prepare him for a greater task.

Moses ran for his life after taking the life of an Egyptian job supervisor. He ran to the backside of the desert to escape from Pharaoh. He was trained in the best of Egyptian schools and customs, but he became a fugitive from justice. He tended the sheep that belonged to Jethro, his father-in-law. Moses stayed in isolation forty years. God spoke to him from a burning bush and re-commissioned him for service. God developed Moses in seclusion, and at the right time when Moses was prepared, God used him to lead the Hebrews out of slavery and into freedom.

Jesus is the supreme illustration of being separated only unto God. He often pulled away from His followers to be alone with His Father. Christ was alone in the garden of Gethsemane, agonizing with the Father as the cross loomed before Him. His disciples slept while He prayed diligently for the will of His Father to be done.

To be captivated alone with God is valuable in working through the grief process. After all, our Lord is the great healer. There is tremendous value in the purpose of God when He places us in solitude and obscurity only with Him. Cherish the moments you have with God. It is then God has your full attention. The people had begun their effort to deal with their loss and grief. They made a confession to God. This is a great place to start as we begin to heal.

As they turned to God, they emptied their hurting soul to Him (verse 20). These are words of deep pain and anguish. The people of Jerusalem are suffering physically and emotionally as they call upon God to be an eyewitness of their distress. The heart of the people was broken and without hope of being repaired. These sufferings are expressions of the severe mental agitation the people encountered.[4] They express grief due to the losses they experienced. There is deep regret for their actions. Verse 22b says, "For my sighs are many, and my heart is faint." The nations surrounding them refused to give comfort. Their laughter at Jerusalem's ruined condition only added to their discomfort.

In verses 21b and 22a, the people of Judah make an unusual request from God. They ask God for revenge upon all those who laughed at their pitiful state. The King James Version says: "Thou wilt bring the day that thou has called, and they shall be like unto me. Let all their wickedness come before thee; and do unto them, as thou has done unto me for all my transgressions."

These verses gain our attention and deserve further interpretation. There are two important truths expressed in these verses. This plea from the people is a reminder that God will not allow any sin to go unpunished. When they pray, "let all their wickedness come before thee," they recognized the truth of God's justice. In fact, Jeremiah spoke of the same punishment being given to Babylonia as they gave to Judah (Jeremiah 25:12-14). The people were praying what they had heard Jeremiah speak previously. Isaiah 10:12 makes mention of God using the king of Assyria to fulfill His will to punish Jerusalem and then God will punish the Assyrians.

It is the latter part of verse 22 that often gives New Testament Christians concern. It is a prayer of revenge upon Judah's enemies. This verse has the fingerprints of Jeremiah upon it, because on several occasions he called upon God to bring vengeance upon those who persecuted him (Jeremiah 11:20, 12:3, 15:15, 17:18, 18:21-23, 20:11).[5] This seemed to be a common practice that people employed in biblical days.

However, it does not fit with the teachings of Jesus Christ when He said in Matthew 5:44, "Love your enemies, bless those who curse you, do good to those who hate you, and pray for those who spitefully use you and persecute you."

One cannot claim that the Old Testament is void of directives to love or show acts of mercy toward your enemies (Proverbs 25:21-22).

There are instructions to do kind deeds to those who oppose you (Exodus 23:4-5). Perhaps we need a reality check at this point. The inhabitants of Jerusalem were being totally honest and human as they expressed their pain. They reacted as a hurting people who seek to hurt other people. They spewed out their bitterness and cried for revenge because pain is in the soul of every broken heart. The cry for revenge is not acceptable to our Lord, but it is raw humanity speaking. The Bible never seeks to cover up the flaws of its characters. It gives us the true story of people including their faults and failures. Honestly, who has not expressed the same message of revenge for those who hurt us? Revenge is not right, but it is what hurting people often seek.

The Rewards of Grief

An effort must be made to find a good route to the road of healing from our grief. What can we do to turn grief into advancement for us? A reminder of a workable definition of grief is necessary at this juncture. Grief is a response to a loss. It is profitable for it shows us how deeply we loved someone or something that is now missing in our lives. Grief is the emotional suffering in a heart that has loved and lost.

There are a variety of types of losses that can lead to grief. The loss could be the loss of a loved one to death or divorce or the loss of a job, a family pet, loss of finances, loss of friendship, or the death of a dream. Even when we change geographical locations, the result is often grief.

Grief interrupts our lives. Grief brings inward pain, and it brings a host of unwelcome guests into our hearts if we do not deal with it in a constructive way. Some of these undesirable associates of grief are anxiety, hurt, anger, negative thoughts, and depression. Grief must be processed in such a way that we can adjust our minds to make changes in our lives as to avoid these unwelcome intruders. Using Lamentations Chapter 1 as our guide, let's ponder the question, "How can we allow

God to use our grief to advance us for His purpose?"

Perhaps it would be helpful to describe some symptoms of grief. As mentioned earlier, I did not recognize my pain as grief until a professional counselor told me. All I knew was that there was a deep gash cut into my soul, and I needed help to get out of the darkness. From the website Healgrief.com, some of these symptoms of grief are listed for our benefit. These serve only as signposts to alert us that we are grieving. Everybody grieves their own way and in their own time. There are no firm, concrete symptoms of grief. So, you may not notice these symptoms; however, that does not mean that you are grieving incorrectly.

The symptoms of grief are as follows: (1) Shock and disbelief, (2) Sadness, (3) Guilt, (4) Anger, (5) Fear, (6) Physical Pain.[6] Many of these symptoms are revealed in Lamentations Chapter 1. For example, verse 1 begins with the exclamation of the word "How." The word is used to express astonishment or shock and disbelief. Today, we might respond by saying, "I cannot believe this is happening to me." There is an expression of numbness to reality. These feelings only prove our humanity. Sadness is a symptom of grief. It is accompanied with a feeling of being alone. Verse 2 recognizes this feeling. The city cries all night and tears chase each other down her cheeks. She feels alone in her grief and mentions that no one is there to comfort her. Sometimes when we feel alone and no one understands our pain, we go into a deeper state of grief. Guilt raises its head as we grieve. We feel guilty over many things. Sometimes the guilt is real, and sometimes it is false. For example, in the death of a loved one, we may place false guilt upon ourselves when we think we could have changed the outcome of the death if we had offered more help or just been there when the loved one died. The truth is, our presence or helpfulness would not have changed the outcome of the experience. Jeremiah writes of the people's expression of guilt in verses 5, 8, 9 and 18. The people of Judah expressed true guilt. They had sinned and brought judgment upon their own leaders.

Anger is another symptom of grief. Anger may be expressed at the person who left you or at the circumstances that caused your loved one to pass. You might even direct your anger at God Himself. In time, the anger will pass and acceptance sets in, but the anger is a sign of your grief. The problem is when we get stuck on the anger, and we do not attempt to work through it or do not know how to move forward. Lamentations Chapter 1, verses 3, 7, 12, 16, 19 and 21 express notes of anger. Fear is another symptom of grief. Fears of the future, of your death and of the unknown are true symptoms of grief. Verse 4 speaks of the lack of a future because the temple is destroyed. The young women who desired a husband and family have become fearful that their dreams will not come true. The people of Jerusalem are fearful that their future is no more promising. Physical pain is another symptom that is expressed in Chapter 1. Verse 6 speaks of being weak from starvation. The fire of judgment burns in Jerusalem's bones. She is sick all the day (13). Her strength is gone, and she is made helpless (14). Verse 20 speaks of the painful emotional status. Jerusalem has a broken heart. Her soul is in pain. Verses 12 and 21 speak of her depth of suffering. God made our bodies, mind and spirit so in touch with each other. When one part of us hurts the other parts are affected, too. Sometimes sheer fatigue sets in and we find it hard to move physically. Sometimes there is a weight gain or loss. Our immune system is in jeopardy, and we are susceptible to illnesses that under normal conditions we would resist. Grief is harsh to the body, mind, and spirit.

As you observe the symptoms of grief you can see that the grief in the people of Judah was real and harsh, and yet God used the grief to build their faith in Him.

For the remainder of this chapter, some of the values of grief will be explored. The wonderful truth is that God never wastes pain. He uses the pain of grief to mature His people into the likeness of Christ. The cold truth is that many of God's children do not grow into His likeness while they are enjoying pleasure and prosperity. God can use the good times of our lives to mature us. Personally speaking, He shapes and develops me in the harsh, painful experiences of life. I agree with C.S. Lewis that "God whispers to us in our pleasures, speaks in our conscience, but shouts in our pain; it is this megaphone to rouse a deaf world."[7] The good news is that in our grief over the losses in life, God is there with us. To be honest, this truth is often said in the context of a faithful heart. The faithful child of God must seek Him and find Him by faith. Here, in the middle of trouble, physical eyes fail us. The eyes of faith see Him who is invisible as we seek after God in our pain (Hebrews 11:6, 27). A close look in Chapter 1 shows there is not any voice response from God. Jeremiah speaks and Jerusalem speaks but God is silent. He gives no guidance, promises or encouragements to Jerusalem. His silence is one way He urges us to pursue Him as we live for Him. The people express maturing faith as they call out to Him.

There are some seasons in the timing of God's wisdom that cause Him to hide His face from His people. Isaiah 45:15 says, "Verily thou art a God that hidest thyself, O God of Israel, the Savior" (KJV). The writings of the Psalms often ask, "Why O Lord do you hide thyself in times of trouble?" (Psalms 10:1, 13:1, 44:24, 88:14 and 89:46). Without a doubt, the people of Jerusalem asked the question, "God, why have You hidden your face from us?" God withdraws from us sometimes to capture our full attention. It is likened to playing hide-and-seek in reverse. The parent is hidden quietly from the child for a moment. The parent is never too far away to help, but the child rushes to find his parent because he feels alone. God temporarily hides His face from us so we will search diligently for Him.

Just because God is silent in our grief does not mean He is

unavailable or inactive. Grief that settles over our heart often makes us feel that God is not present. We try to pray, but we feel that God is so very far from us. It is difficult to encounter God when grief paralyzes the heart. In such times, what we are experiencing by way of feelings must be replaced by the fact of faith. God has promised His constant presence. He is there with you and in you even during the times you think He is far removed.

The people of Jerusalem serve as our example, for they responded to their loss and grief with a call unto God to confess their wrongs and acknowledge His righteousness (verse 20). During times of grief run to God. Bare your soul to Him. Renew your faith in Him. Gain His strength from being in His presence. The loss that God allows to occur can eventually work for good if we run to Him with our broken lives. God does speak through our grief, and it serves as an invitation to return to God in confession and fellowship. Through the grief a more mature relationship may develop with Him.

Lamentations 1:13 uses the phrase "hath turned me back" (KJV). The term that Jeremiah used means to "repent" or "come all the way back" to God. God will use the grief to turn Judah from her sins to God.

God knows exactly what to allow into our lives to cause us to turn all the way back to Him. He will lovingly allow hurts and hardships to gain our attention and return us to Him. In the case of Judah, it was the destruction of Jerusalem and deportation of citizens from the country. For us, He might use the loss of a job, bank account or relationship to usher us back to Him. He will not allow any rivals in our lives. We must be aware that God's greatest desire for us is not that we become happy, healthy or wealthy, but that we become holy like Him. His passion for us is that we conform to Him. God will remove whatever stands in our way of becoming Christ-like. God is not being unkind as He does so. He simply loves our fellowship with Him more than the objects in our lives that hinder our union with Him.

Another contribution is that suffering develops us into Christlikeness (verse 12). The heartfelt cry from the hurting people asks her neighbors, "Is it nothing to you, all you who pass by?" Behold and see if there is any sorrow like my sorrow. It is believed the language here prefigures Christ more than Jerusalem. Harry Ironside, in his book *Lamentations and Jeremiah*, agrees that the verse is prophetic in reference to Christ on the cross.[8] No one suffered as Christ. He suffered not for His sin but for the sins of the world. He was a "Man of Sorrows."

There is nothing that will put you on the highway to Christlikeness like suffering, both physical and emotional. Paul the Apostle wrote the following in Philippians 3:10: "That I may know Him and the power of His resurrection, and the fellowship of His sufferings, being conformed to His death."

The desire of every true believer is to develop into the likeness of our Lord (Romans 8:29). However, all believers do not desire to surrender to His demands to do so. We want to experience the power of His resurrection, yet no one is willing to die. We desire more personal knowledge of Him, yet we are not willing to pass through the gauntlet of suffering, rejection, and death as He did.

Perhaps we are never more like Christ than when we suffer pain and loss. It is in those moments when our hearts are crushed as grapes in a winepress that we pray with total attention on Him. Only when we are so wounded in the recesses of our spirit can we cry out and plead our cause for His healing. Only when we get so desperate will we find His presence satisfying. At some point and time, all who seek to know Christ on a deeper level will experience a Gethsemane moment. It is in that hour when we have come to the end of our abilities and wisdom that we find ourselves alone like Christ and the people of Jerusalem. Then we are real before God. It is then that we can identify with Christ and the fellowship of His suffering.

Our Lord was no stranger to being rejected by foe, friend, and family. He knew what it was to be considered "out of His mind" because His mission in life was different from others. He knew what it was to be forsaken by His disciples in the time of His trial and death. He knew how it felt to be misjudged, ridiculed, and lied about through the rumors people spread. He knew what it felt like to lose a friend and cry at his grave. In fact, there is not one thing that our Lord failed to experience while on earth. Therefore, when we suffer grief due to losses in life, we can understand that Christ has a plan to mold us into Christlikeness as we identify with Him.

Notes

1. Walter C. Kaiser, *A Biblical Approach to Personal Suffering* (Eugene: Wipf & Stock Publishers, 1980), 10.

2. Notes in New King James Version (Nashville: Holman Publishers, 1982), 719.

3. F.B. Huey Jr., *The New American Commentary* (Nashville: Broadman Press, 1993), 455.

4. Kaiser, *A Biblical Approach to Personal Suffering*, 55.

5. Huey Jr., *The New American Commentary*, 457.

6. "Common Symptoms of Grief," https://healgrief.org/common-symptoms-grief

7. C.S. Lewis, *The Complete C.S. Lewis Signature Classics* (New York: Harper Collins Publishers, 2002), 91.

8. H.A. Ironside, *Lamentations and Jeremiah*, (Neptune: Loizeaux Brothers, 1973), 314.

Chapter 2
Pain of Grief

Chapter 2 of the Book of Lamentations is not written for those who are weak of heart. The chapter reveals a dark and somewhat depressing scene of God's wrath as it is "thrown down" upon the city of Jerusalem. Within this chapter, a side of God's character is presented that is seldom spoken of from today's pulpits. The wrath of God has been released against Jerusalem. He shows no mercy as He removes His protective hand from the people and uses His might to fight with Judah's enemy.

Although Chapter 2 is very similar to Chapter 1, there is a distinct difference. The people have spurned God's call to repentance from their disobedience and rebellion against His commands. His patience has worn out. His punishment is ferocious and deliberate. God is angry! He is not taking their sinfulness anymore.

Jeremiah speaks of God in half of the verses in Chapter 2. God is credited with the total destruction of the city and everything else that has fallen on the city. As in Chapter 1, the first verse begins with the word "How," which introduces a funeral lament. As a dark cloud would cover an area, God's anger hovered above Jerusalem. Like a star falling from the heavens, so did beautiful Jerusalem fall from her glory. God's anger was so fierce that not even His "footstool" was spared. The "footstool" may be the temple or the ark of the covenant (1 Chronicles 28:2; Psalm 132:7). The statements, "daughters of Zion," "glory of Israel," and "His footstool," are probably progressive in nature. Daughters of Zion speaks of the people of the nation. The "glory of Israel" speaks of the city — Jerusalem. As stated above, "His footstool" is either the temple or the ark of the covenant. However, one can note how God's anger increases upon Judah. Everything is included in the judgment. Nothing is too precious to be spared. Make no mistake, the destruction of the city was allowed because God was angry at the sinfulness of the people.

Therefore, verses 2-10 present to the reader the description of God's destruction on the nation as a result of God's anger. Verses 2-5 display God's anger directed at the entire nation of Judah. Throughout verses 6-8, Jeremiah describes God's anger at Jerusalem. Verses 9 and 10 give to the reader a view of the destruction of the temple.

Beginning in Chapter 2, verse 2, God "swallows up" the people of Jacob. The word "swallow" means to "consume" or to "utterly destroy" and occurs also in verses 5, 8 and 16.[1] God exercises no pity as He "throws down" His wrath upon the people. He destroys their houses as well as their "strongholds." These were the landmarks of their safety, such as the palaces, castles, citadels and watchtowers. These places were brought level to the ground and so were their rulers.

Verse 3 speaks of "His anger" as God "cut off the horn of Israel." The word "horn" refers to the nation's strength (Jeremiah 48:25). God is featured as withdrawing "His right hand" of power as the enemy of Judah approaches. God will not help Judah, nor will He hinder the Babylonian army from destroying the country. The fire of God's judgment will burn among them, and without God, Judah has no strength to protect herself.

The reason for Judah's inability to defend herself is understood in verses 4-5. God is against Judah. He is acting as their enemy. Scripture says, "The Lord was like an enemy," as He engaged in warfare against Judah (verse 5). "Standing like an enemy, He has bent His bow; with His right hand, like an adversary" (verse 4). The use of the phrases "like an enemy" and "like an adversary" are used to show how distressing this fact is to the people. Some commentators believe that God has become a real enemy to Judah. Other commentators believe this is only to express His acting as an enemy. God was never an actual enemy of Judah. Either way, God allowed the army of Nebuchadnezzar to destroy "all that were pleasant to the eye in the tabernacle of the daughter of Zion." The finest young men of Judah's army were slain by the archers of the Babylonian army. This may also include the deaths of the wives and children and key leaders of the fallen nation which are described as the "daughters of Zion." The Lord totally consumed Judah. Her palaces were destroyed, and the people mourned over these happenings.

In verses 6-8, Jeremiah describes the aggression that God turns on Jerusalem. God destroyed the tabernacle and made waste of it as a plowed garden. Even the tabernacle, a place of worship, wasn't spared regardless of her glory. The items that were associated with the worship center were taken away. The holy days were forgotten. The altar was destroyed. The work of the priest and king was no longer needed. God leveled both the political and religious systems because they were filled with corruption and shallow worship and were of no value to God or the country. Shouts of victory and celebration from the invaders filled the air. The nation that was hated by her enemies has now succumbed to the ground in defeat.

Verses 8-10 complete the paragraph that deals with the destruction of the temple. Again, the language is very descriptive. The anger of God is being expressed as He has drawn off the temple with a measuring line and marked it for destruction. There is a note of deep gloom in verse 9 when it states, "[T]he law is no more; and her prophets find no vision from the Lord." God would no longer use the king or priest to give guidance to the people. God's anger was at full throttle, and His fiery judgment was at full blast. Even the city gates were destroyed. The heat of God's fury was white hot, and the city suffered many losses because of their sin. The wise leaders of Jerusalem have no advice to give. They sit with sackcloth and dust upon their heads to show their grief. The young maidens hang their heads. They, too, have lost their hope for a better day.

The second major paragraph in Chapter 2 features verses 11-17. Here the desperation of the prophet is very apparent to the reader. Jeremiah opens up his soul for us to see his hurting heart. He joins with the people and shares in their grief of losing so much. He speaks of his inner pain in verse 11 as he says, "[M]y bowels are troubled, my liver is poured upon the earth" (KJV). The ancients believed that the bowels and liver (i.e., heart) were the center places of human emotions. Jeremiah was full of brokenhearted misery. Jeremiah above anyone else poured his life into informing the people of their need to repent. He had warned day and night of the coming judgment of God unless they turned back to God. He had exhausted himself in turning the people away from idolatry. No doubt, he is heartbroken for now he sees firsthand the display of the anger of God.

Jeremiah sees small children starving to death in the streets and in their mothers' arms. This is just too much for his emotional health to bear. The sights are unbearable. His memory of times past was that of happy children playing, laughing with great joy with their faces full of life. Jeremiah is known as the weeping prophet. Here, he cries tears of sorrow for the suffering people. He understands their tears. The truth that Jeremiah must face is that the innocents often are the victims of others' sins.

Jeremiah is aware of the hopelessness of people all around him. He responds as one who is living a horror story in real time. There in the streets, Jeremiah hears the sounds of starving people crying out for food yet without hope of being fed (verse 12). Death is all around and hopelessness fills the air. Jeremiah's spirit is broken and poured out upon the ground. He has emptied himself before the people as he urged them to repent.

Verse 13 shows us the compassion Jeremiah has toward the people experiencing such hurt. He acknowledges the gaping wound is deeply entrenched in their lives. He realizes that he has no ability to help. There are times when we want to ease someone's pain, but we are unable to do so. Only God can help people in this situation. In other words, when God crushes someone, only God can bring healing. Therefore, when God judges someone they must return to Him, for only He can rebuild their life.

Jeremiah turns to blame the false prophets for their part in the devastation of Judah (verse 14). They were the ones who misled the people by whitewashing the truth of God's call to repentance and of God's promise of judgment if there was no repentance. The false prophets answered the people that God would not punish them because they were "His very own people." Therefore, they simply lied and offered empty promises of hope. These professional charlatans of prophecy should have told the truth while there was time for the people to repent. As a result, the people listened to the easy sound of their messages and continued on the downward path to destruction. Now those who travel past the city mock the hurting people by clapping their hands, hissing, and wagging their heads. They shout in celebration over Jerusalem's fall in verses 15 and 16.

Verse 17 is the key verse of Chapter 2. Although Jeremiah was correct in casting blame at the false prophets for not being honest in warning Judah of the judgment, there is deeper truth to consider. The truth is that the destruction of the city was in the plan of God since ancient days (Leviticus 26:14-45; Deuteronomy 28:15-68; Jeremiah 51:12; Zechariah 1:6). God allowed the enemies to celebrate their victory over the city. From the very beginning, the fall of the nation, collapse of the city, and the fall of the temple was in the plan of God. The devastation was something new to the nation, but God had this act planned since the beginning of time. What wonderful wisdom that God displays.

Often the issue surfaces that God made a covenant to protect His people. Yes, but the covenant was based upon the people always being obedient and faithful to Him. The breaking of the covenant was upon the people, not upon God. God merely fulfilled His promise by allowing the enemy to destroy the nation. The King James Version is very strong in the language as it states, "The Lord hath done that which He had devised." The New Living Translation states, "But it is the Lord who did just as He planned." The enemy was victorious, and the crowd of onlookers mocked with glee, yet they did not understand that God permitted this work through them. They took credit, but it was all of God's might and will.

More will be said of verse 17 later in this chapter. For now, a close look at verses 18-22 gives us some directions for returning to God.

Jeremiah instructs the people to cry out to God in earnest prayer. He expresses a note of deep desperation as he calls upon the people to cry out to God and to show them pity because of their suffering (verse 18). Jerusalem was encouraged to pray without rest and with unceasing tears flowing from their eyes (verse 18). It is not clear whether the people were to cry for relief from suffering or to cry tears of repentance toward God. Jeremiah continues his instructions to the people to pray during the night. They were to pour out their hearts like waterfalls unto God. The night was divided into three watches of four hours per watch. The people were to pray at the beginning of each watch. They expressed their pain with tears, prayers and broken hearts as they lifted their hands in worship to God (verse 19).

Grief and prayer are often companions in the losses of life. The first step in the healing process is that of sincere prayer that bears the broken soul to God and pleads for grace and healing. In those dark times of grief, prayer — along with tears — expresses to God a brokenness that only God can understand. It is during that time one realizes that the pain resulting from loss in life is too great for them, so they invite the God of all comfort to join with them in the grieving process. It is comforting to know that God is there with us all along, and He welcomes us to tell Him of our deepest loss and grief. This is the first step in returning to God.

There are differences of opinion as to who actually is praying in verses 20-22. Perhaps the best understanding is that the city is praying in response to the instruction by Jeremiah.[2] The people voice their concerns before God. They remind God that He is the one who allowed this devastation. He chose to punish His people with such injury, yet He did not punish the pagan nations. The question is accusatory in nature as they ask, "O Lord, ... should You treat Your own people this way?" (NLT).

The people understood that God is sovereign. He punishes sin because of His love for holiness and hatred for sin. God is in control of all present and past happenings. Therefore, God is the One who is credited with causing these horrible events (verse 21). They accuse God of three deliberate catastrophes in their country. Number one, they accuse God of permitting such starvation that women, who by nature give life and nurture children, have now become cannibals. The famine was so great that they became desperate and their most depraved nature was displayed. Also, the priests were slain in all places in the sanctuary. They would say, "God, you did nothing to stop these atrocities. Number two, God is accused by the people of expressing His anger and allowing men and women of all ages to be killed by the enemy. They said of the Lord that He showed no mercy (verse 21). Number three, they accused God of being guilty because He used the enemies of Judah to carry forth His judgment upon His people. There are two pictures in verse 22 that illustrate this truth. There is the picture of a priest who announces a religious gathering — a feast day — and as the gathering proceeds, the enemy comes and encircles the city to bring terror on every side. The next picture is of the city speaking as a mother who cares for her dead child. It is a sad story of how no one, including the innocent child, is spared from the wrath of God.

The prayer of the people ceases. God responds with silence. In other words, He gives no response. The pleas and questions to God concerning their suffering and grief and their accusations of God's involvement are left before God.

One can easily understand why the Book of Lamentations is not the most popular Bible study among students of Scripture. The story line of the book is sad. Chapter 2 leaves the reader with depressing thoughts. If one stops reading at Chapter 2, he is met with the grim truth that the people of Judah are without hope as they suffer under the raging and violent anger of God.

One difference between Chapter 1 and Chapter 2 is that there is an expression of a deeper level of grief in Chapter 2. The losses of the country are legion. There are losses on many personal fronts. There are losses in religious and political systems. There is a loss of hope as the younger generation lay dead in the streets. In all of their losses, there is not yet a cry of genuine repentance and return to God. There are, however, accusations leveled at God for causing this chaos in their lives. There seems to be some anger toward God for this trouble in the people's lives.

What are the lessons concerning grief from this chapter that we can learn? In the midst of all the darkness, several rays of light can be observed.

As previously stated, within the verses of Chapter 2, there is a strong emphasis upon prayer as it relates to grief. Jeremiah saw the devastation around the people. He knew that he could not "fix" these conditions. However, he did know that God could "fix" their broken lives. Jeremiah did what men of God do. He pointed them to God. He told them to "cry aloud before the Lord (verse 18, NLT). Through passionate prayer they could express their sorrow to God. Prayer is a mighty avenue whereby we can find comfort during grief.

Prayer is one way that we can express our inner pain to God and admit our need to Him. In these moments of prayer, we find the solace to admit our need to God and recognize that His mighty power is greater than ourselves and our circumstances. God, through prayer, has the ability to change our perspective on life. He gives hope to us in the darkest of trials in life. As one humbles himself in the presence of God, He reveals at least two wonderful truths to us that are often hidden behind the cloud of grief. Number one, when you have nothing else to hold to that provides comfort, you still have God. Ron Dunn, the great pastor and Bible teacher, once said that he has been to the bottom of life and found the bottom to be rock. The rock is Jesus. In Christ, you discover that He is sufficient to take care of all your needs and comfort your hurting heart. Number two, you will discover that He continues to love you, and He can be trusted. This truth will allow you to accept that He has allowed this grief for a reason that might be known only to Him. This acceptance and trust in God will allow you to pray as Christ did in the Garden of Gethsemane, "Not my will but thine be done." This is a prayer that expresses absolute confidence in God who has a plan for your life, and He is working out that plan for your best interest and for His glory (Romans 8:28).

Experiencing grief is a roller coaster ride that invokes many emotions. There are several stages of the grief process that will be mentioned later in this writing. One of the many emotions is anger. Anger during grief can be directed at oneself, at loved ones, and, of course, at God. In fact, God is often the target of this anger. The common response when one is angry at God is to stop communicating with Him. This is tragic because prayer keeps us connected to God. There is great wisdom in encouraging one to pray as they grieve even if they "feel" that God is silent. God is the greatest healer in our grief. He gives strength to navigate through the rough road to healing from our grief. Talking to God as we grieve is so necessary to bring inner healing from a broken heart. In full honesty, there are times in our grief when all we can do is pray. And sometimes, we cannot even do that. But even in times we cannot pray, we know God understands. He is with us when life hurts so badly.

Often tears will go in tandem with prayer. There is great value in expressing oneself through tears. The psalmist wrote in Chapter 56, verse 8, "You number my wanderings; put my tears into your bottle; are they not in your book?" These are comforting words that convey to us that God knows of our journey. We may not know where we have been or where we are in life, but God has kept an account. Our tears have been too many at times to number, but our considerate and compassionate Lord has a record of all of them, and He has kept them in His bottle. Not a tear falls from our eye that does not catch the attention of our Lord.

Tears are a gift from God that allow us the ability to speak of our grief through a language that everyone can understand. Jeremiah understood the power of tears, for he tells the people to "let your tears flow like a river day and night" (verse 18). When our words fail to express our deepest emotions, tears are the words that show others our inner pain. Tears speak for us when we are hurting too much to talk. You might say that tears are words in liquid form. As you grieve, give yourself permission to cry. Why withhold the wonderful gift that God gave in tears to wash away inward pain? People who think they must be strong just to maintain an image for someone else are placing upon themselves an unnecessary burden along with existing grief. Tears are a human response to grief and sorrow.

Our greatest example of the power of tears is in the person of Jesus. He stands at the tomb of Lazarus, His friend, and He weeps. There are many suggestions as to why Jesus wept, but forgive me for stating the obvious. Our Lord wept because His friend had died. He shows His humanity because He grieves at the death of His friend. Our Lord understands every tear that rolls down the cheeks of those who grieve, and He gives us permission to cry because He too wept.

Ken Gire writes, "[S]o much is distilled in our tears, not the least of which is wisdom in living life. From my own tears I have learned that if you follow your tears, you will find your heart. If you find your heart, you will find what is dear to God. And, if you find what is dear to God, you will find the answer to how you should live your life."[3]

In time the tears of any loss will pass. Ultimately, God will wipe away all our tears from our eyes (Revelation 2:14, KJV). For now, you might be passing through the valley of tears. Remember the psalmist, for he wrote in Psalm 126:5: "Those who sow with tears will reap with songs of joy" (NIV). For the present time, give yourself some grace and permission to be human and cry.

Within Chapter 2, there is a wonderful observation of the person of God. God is gracious and kind to those of His family to allow us a small revelation of His nature as we pass through the dark days of grief. Sadly, our understanding of God's truth and His character comes during the painful times in our lives. God can and does grow us in the good times of our lives, but He finds that we are most eager to learn in our trials. There are two themes concerning His character. In Chapter 2, His anger is highlighted as well as His sovereignty. How do these two characteristics of God's nature play out in grief?

The subject of God's anger is heavily emphasized in Chapter 2. The anger/wrath of God (there is little difference in these words except wrath can be understood as a more intensified word for anger) is the result of the wickedness of the people of Judah. The most common Hebrew term for anger is *aph,* which denotes either human or divine anger. The term refers to nostril, which the ancients thought to be the locale of anger.[4] The word *anap* denotes the anger of God (to breathe hard). The King James Version uses the wording "His anger" five times and certainly draws our attention. The phrase is used in verses 1, 3, 6, 21 and 22. The phrase "His wrath" is used in verse 2, and "His fury" is used in verse 4. Because this term is a repeated so often, perhaps it is worthy of a closer study.

In his book *Knowing God*, J.I. Packer is helpful in understanding God's wrath as His adverse reaction to evil, which is a necessary part of his moral perfection. Therefore, when God unleashes His anger, His justice, holiness and righteousness are on display. Packer underscores the truth that when humanity feels the blast of God's wrath, it is because humanity has retreated from the light that God offers and run into darkness.[5]

There is a strange silence today from many pulpits concerning the subject of the anger of God. The attributes of God's anger are surrendered for a softer view of God as a wonderful grandfather, too loving to express His nature of wrath. However, this is not the view of the Bible. In Nahum 1:2-8, God's wrath is one of His many attributes. The subject of God's anger should not lessen our opinion of Him, but should enforce a deeper respect for Him. If God did not become angry at those who practice sin, He would cease to be holy for He would permit sin to go unpunished.

God's anger is unlike human anger. God is not "mad" as some would define someone who has lost their mental reasoning. Nor is God presenting Himself as a playground bully proving His strength by being cruel to humanity. God is not unpredictable. He does not become "moody" or haphazard in expressing His anger. The ways we describe human anger cannot be employed to describe the anger of God. God never uses anger without good reason. Only God is just. Therefore, out of His character of justice, He will show anger against those who are unjust (Romans 2:5-6). God is fair and perfect in His treatment of every person. He will never have to apologize for mistreating anyone. God's anger does not void His wonderful love for humanity. God's love for people cannot be debated (John 3:16). He has a love for people that is selfless, for He reaches out to people in the person of His Son, Jesus Christ. His love is surrendering. He allowed His Son to be sacrificed for the sins of all people. His love is compassionate as a shepherd who seeks after a lost sheep that has wandered from His flock. His love is correcting for He loves people too much to allow sin to destroy their lives. He loves holiness more than sin, and He loves the sinner more than sin. He loves humanity so much that His nature of holiness will respond in anger against sin as well as the sinner.

It is helpful to know that God did not change His character between the Old and New Testaments. There is ample evidence of God's anger expressed in the New Testament (John 3:36, Romans 1:18, Revelation 19:15). Jesus displayed His anger at those who used the house of God to make a profit from the worshipers who traveled great distances to Jerusalem. His anger moved Him to correct an injustice. Paul the apostle taught us to "be angry and sin not." Anger is valuable when it motivates a person to correct a wrong and when it incites a person to behave in a righteous way. There is biblical support for anger when it is employed for the above reasons. Anger is never pleasing to God when used for personal revenge. God is completely justified in His anger toward iniquity.

There is a stark contrast between the anger of God toward the unconverted sinner and the child of God. J.I. Packer says:

> Between us sinners and the thunder clouds of divine wrath stands the cross of the Lord Jesus. If we are Christ's through faith then we are justified through His cross and the wrath will never touch us, neither here nor hereafter. Jesus delivers us from the wrath to come (1 Thessalonians 1:10).[6]

The Christian will not experience hell for Christ has paid for our sin by His atoning work on the cross (Romans 3:25-26, 5:9). There is no condemnation to them which are in Christ Jesus (Romans 8:1).

Although the believer in Christ will never experience the wrath of God, He will nevertheless experience the chastisement of God. Hebrews 12:5-11 teaches us that God disciplines His children for the purposes of correction and instruction regarding how not to sin. This act of chastisement from God is proof of a true relationship between God and His child. God's chastening hand upon the people teaches submission, reverence, and obedience toward Him. Also, through chastisement the child of God learns to hate sin and love holiness.

Below is a chart to help us understand the differences between the wrath of God upon the unconverted and the chastisement of God upon His child.

Wrath of God upon the sinner	**Chastisement of God upon the saint**
Purpose: To inflict a penalty because of wickedness	Purpose: To train and to correct
Focus: To punish the sinner	Focus: Maturing growth toward Christ-likeness
Progress: Wrath, judgment	Progress: Holy lifestyle, obedience, hatred of sin, love for holiness
Result: Fear, hopelessness, hell	Result: Heaven, life purpose, life fulfillment

How does the anger/wrath of God upon the sinner and the chastisement of God upon the saint affect our grief?

Grief is an emotion that can be very inconsistent. One day you might feel as though you have passed through the pain, but then the next day you find yourself battling the pain again. There is a time of consistency where all is well. Then, out of the blue, there is a picture, or a sound, a letter that will cause your mind to be flooded with an element of grief. Those who face this yo-yo effect of grief yearn for some stability that will afford them a peaceful life. They need something to count on that is sure and steadfast, which can give them confidence that can be depended on when their world is rocked with grief.

The answer is not found in things of this life, but in the person of God. The good side of this characteristic of God is that He is consistent. He is stable. The anger/chastisement of God is an expression of His holy and just nature. He does not punish some and close His eyes to others' sin. God does not condone in the life of a saint what He condemns in the life of the sinner. He is fair. He causes the rain to fall on the just and unjust. He is trustworthy. He is true to His word. The person who is in the midst of grief can find confidence in Him because His actions will remain true to His nature. God is consistent. His nature, His love, mercy, compassion, and care are consistent as well. He never fails to give love and grace to those in need. God can be counted on in times when our hearts are hurt by grief.

The anger and chastisement of God is valuable to those who grieve because He reveals a part of Himself that many people never grasp. He can be one who punishes sin. Whenever God chooses to reveal Himself to us, we are most privileged. He has a future for us. He has a plan that He has designed for us to fulfill. There is hope! He is still active in our life.

God's anger, as well as chastisement, has the power to correct our actions and attitudes toward sin. God's punishment/correction in our lives is painful. We often lose things that we have allowed to become first place in our lives instead of God. The result of the loss is grief. Out of a broken heart, we may be humbled and realize that God can heal us and that He loves us. We begin to understand that God's love for us is leading us to repentance.

It must be said very clearly, as well as dogmatically, that every sickness and loss and problem that befalls us is not because of unrepentant sin. We live in a sin-cursed, broken, and twisted world. This world is fertile ground for all forms of disease, death, and deformity. People of faith as well as people without faith in Christ get sick. They become invalid. They lose relationships and eventually lose their lives. These are the results that come from living in this world. We are not to be judges of people's sickness or trials. However, we must not overlook the truth that through God's loving character He expresses His anger toward sinners and His discipline toward the saints so that we will turn to Him in repentance. God is not limited in the means at His disposal to bring us to Himself. During times of loss, we would be wise to stop, look, and listen for His plea to us. Perhaps this is an excellent time to ask God what is He saying to us? What is God teaching us through these painful experiences? This expression of God's anger/chastisement is a call for us to confess our sins, repent from our sins, and run to God (1 John 1:9). His expression of anger/chastisement can show us His consistent nature and His love for people so that we can praise Him, as the psalmist said in 119:71, "It is good for me that I have been afflicted, that I may learn Your statutes."

The first characteristic of God is His wrath. Jeremiah shows us the characteristic of God's anger in the first section in Chapter 2. The second characteristic of God's person is found in verse 17: "The Lord has done what He purposed; He has fulfilled His word which He commanded in days of old. He has thrown down and has not pitied, and He has caused an enemy to rejoice over you; He has exalted the horn of your adversaries."

Verse 17 is the key verse of Chapter 2. This verse exposes two truths concerning God's personhood. Since God is the key figure of Chapter 2, the study of His character is in order. God's honesty is revealed. As far back as the day of Moses, God made it clear that judgment would come upon the people if they forsook Him (Leviticus 26:14-39). God used Jeremiah as a mouthpiece to remind His people of the coming judgment if they failed to repent. The choice of the people was to reject God's call. God's choice was to keep His promise and send judgment.

The honesty of God is a certainty to a troubled heart. God cannot lie for it is against His character. The troubled heart can find great strength in the promises of God's word to equip it to heal from grief. Like Him, His word never fails.

Permit me to give you a personal example of holding on to a promise of God. In my studies I had read through and preached from the minor prophet Joel. (Reminder: Joel is a minor prophet only in the sense of his brevity and not his message.) After being stuck in my grief from so many personal and professional losses and finding no relief from depression, hope, for me, was a rare virtue. One morning as I sat in my study, I opened the writings of Joel and began to read. To be honest, I first thought that this little book would have nothing for me, yet I proceeded to read. I read through Chapter 1 without a bit of excitement. I continued into Chapter 2. Then I read verse 25, and lights, bells and whistles went off in my inner-being. It says: "And I will restore to you the years that the locust hath eaten, the cankerworm, and the caterpillar, and the palmerworm, my great army which I sent among you" (KJV).

Somehow, I saw that verse for the first time in such a way that it jumped off the page into my heart. I am sure I had read it prior to this, but this time it was for me. I realized that some will say, "The verse is only a promise to Judah and not to a Christian in modern times." I disagree. I took it as a personal message of hope from God to my life and my grief. It spoke words of healing, recovery, and renewal of my life in the future, and that is what I needed at that time in my journey of grief. I needed to know that I have reason to hope for a day that God will restore the years, the experiences that I missed, the opportunities I had failed to grasp because I was stuck in a grief holding pattern. God's word said to me, "Here is hope for a better future; recovery is on the way." I pray that I will never forget that emotional day as Joel 2:25 became my promise verse.

Since that morning I have committed part of that verse to memory. I have a handwritten note to myself on my office board. I have used it to help many troubled couples to have hope that God can restore what they have lost in their marriage because of conflict. It has served others who have lost hope of a better future because of a broken past. I found a poem in my reading that goes alongside of my promise verse. It reads as follows:

> "Grow old along with me
> The best is yet to be
> The last of life for
> which the first was made" — Robert Browning[7]

As time has passed from that early morning reading, I have added other precious promises from God that have renewed by broken spirit. Here are a few that give us confidence in the honesty of God's character.

Psalm 103:5-7
Psalm 71:20-21
Jeremiah 32:17, 42
Jeremiah 33:3
Philippians 4:7, 9, 19
Psalm 46:1
Isaiah 40:29-31
Isaiah 41:10
Isaiah 43:2
Micah 7:8

There is healing power in the mind as one clings dearly to the promises of God. I speak from experience that God's word is true for God is truth. His word will be carried forth. So, trust Him. Trust His truth in times of loss and grief. He never fails.

Verse 17 presents to us another part of God's personhood as God the sovereign. In simple language, the sovereignty of God is His absolute rule over all His creation and creatures. God has no rivals in the universe. Within verse 17, God allowed the destruction of Judah out of His good purpose. He permitted the enemies of Judah to carry out His wrath upon His people. These actions were all a part of God's sovereign will.

Without a doubt the biggest hurdle that Christians face is the "why" question concerning God's absolute sovereign control. Questions such as, "Why does God allow such horrible events?" If God is in control of all the universe and if He loves us, why does He not stop the pain in people's lives?" "Why does God use our enemies to punish us?" These questions are as old as the history of humanity. God is at times presented as one who causes the trouble in peoples' lives (1 Samuel 4:3, 16:14; Isaiah 45:7). The following verses affirm God's sovereignty over humanity.[8] This truth is also seen in the life of Job. Job was a God-fearing man. In one day, his life was turned upside down as he lost his family, farm, and his health. Why did this godly man suffer so harshly? God allowed Satan to test Job in every area, except the taking of Job's life. All along, God was in control. God never surrendered His authority. He limited Satan in his attacks upon Job.

There is no one who can give sufficient answers to the "why" questions of life. As Chapter 1 ends, there are questions from Jeremiah, but God gives no answers. God in His wisdom has not told us everything we would like to know, but He has told us enough to give us faith in Him. Sometimes God remains silent when we have questions. That is part of God's mysterious character. I have discovered a wonderful truth in the silence of God in my questions. He may do something greater than answer my feeble questions. He may show me a new revelation of Himself.

One comforting truth that we can grasp is that there is no experience that is beyond the control of God. God has a plan for individuals as well as the universe, and He is working His plan. We can be confident that God knows of our experiences in life. We may not understand or enjoy what He allows to come to us. He does not have to reveal His blueprints for our lives, nor does He have to seek our approval. Our responsibility is to trust Him with the details and trust that His plan for us is His best for us. When we can accept this, we will feel the weights of worry fall from our minds, and His peace will then fill us with great assurance.

Along this journey of life, we soon discover that the road is not paved with beautiful flowers and soothing music. There are potholes, stop signs, and detours all along the way. There are moments of pain, fear, and confusion. These emotions are common to everyone. The motivation that moves us onward is the confidence that God is in control. He will never allow the setbacks in life to hinder His ultimate plan for our life.

Within the study of the sovereignty of God, there is the conflict of the free will of man. I understand that some say there is no conflict between divine sovereignty and human freedom, but there is a conflict between God's sovereignty and human autonomy.[9] Whatever the choice of words, man is at liberty to choose the lifestyle he desires. There are limits to freedom if one desires to be a productive, well-adjusted person in society. Without restrictions in freedom, the liberty can become an uncontrolled addiction that leads to personal downfall. A person can be free to choose, but he is not free to forgo his choice as to the lifestyle he will live. The people of Judah made a choice to reject the teachings and warnings of God. They were well aware of the results of their choice. They knew if they lived rebellious lives before God, judgment would come. God gave them a choice to honor Him and be blessed or reject

His truth and experience His anger. They chose the way of personal gratification and in so doing chose His wrath. Such is life for it is made up of choices and consequences.

I certainly do not want to be guilty of imposing my own interpretation of the text as I read verses 20-22. I do not want to read too much into Jeremiah's words. I do think there is a lot of personal anger that Jeremiah expresses to God. Jeremiah is revealing his humanity. He suffers as his people suffer. He has allowed himself to enter into their pain, loss, and grief. He feels with them and for them. Kaiser calls this empathic suffering.[10] Grief affects not only those who are personally involved in the pain, but it also affects others. Out of his pain for the people, Jeremiah calls out to God. Who else could he address his concerns to? After all, it was God who was ultimately responsible for this destruction. Jeremiah raises questions to God. He wants answers, and God is silent.

What Jeremiah is doing in these two verses is more than having a temper tantrum. He is searching for God to give him some answers for the suffering of the people. Grief has a way of forcing us to look deeply into our thoughts about life, death, and God. This leads us to a crisis of faith. Here, we raise questions, when in times of comfort we would never ask in public. Thankfully, Jeremiah asks some of these questions for us. For example, "See, O Lord, and consider! To whom have you done this? Should the women eat their offspring, the children they have cuddled? Should the priest and prophet be slain in the sanctuary of the Lord?" (verse 20). Jeremiah seems to be angry with God.

Anger is a part of the grieving process. People allow their anger to be fired off in various directions. Those who experience the death of a loved one get angry at the doctor and hospital for not performing up to expectation. The one recently divorced blames their mate or some other person who may be involved. Anger is like a shotgun blast with pellets that go off in many directions, and often "anger pellets" hit many targets.

Anger directed at someone, at something, or at God is a response to pain that is inside of your soul. The pain is a response of losing something that you loved very much. H. Norman Wright, in his book *Experiencing Grief*, says, "Anger in grief is often in protest, a desire to make someone pay, to declare the unfairness of the death when we were frustrated, hurt, afraid, feeling helpless."[11] The expression of anger can range from an immediate explosion to a quiet withdrawal from people and activities. Wright says that anger can turn against you as it gets stuck in your mind. This leads to depression when the anger is turned inward and not released.

Too often people's anger is directed at God because He allowed the tragedy to happen in their lives. It is this anger toward God that claims my attention. Why is it that people get angry at God? There are as many reasons as there are people, but perhaps there is one common denominator in many cases. People often feel that God has betrayed them. The story unfolds somewhat like this: You have lived an upright life before God. You believe that God can do all things, and you pray with faith over a situation in your life that is troubling you. You have Scripture verses to prove that God will hear and answer your specific and faithful prayer and relieve you of this difficult situation. You might begin to make claims that you have heard from God. Within your mind, you are quite confident that this trying situation in your life will be solved in the specific way that you asked God. However, as time passes, God does not answer the specific way you asked. Your marriage mate leaves and files for divorce, rather than remaining in the relationship. Your close friend or family member dies, when you just knew God said that he would live and regain health. Your rival landed the job you believed you would get. Inside of your heart you ask God questions such as: *Why did You not do as I asked? I did everything right. I prayed with faith. I trusted Your word to me, and You failed me. I revealed to others what You told me. You have made me out as a foolish liar. God, You failed me. How can I ever trust You again?*

This type of experience is common and so is the response of anger toward God. I know. I have been there. If you have not, you are in the minority. Much of our anger at God comes because of unfulfilled expectations. Sometimes we desire something so much that we read our desires as the word of God. When God responds differently from what we have asked, we become angry at Him for not meeting our preconceived ideas of how He should act. Anger toward God sets into our heart when our real-life experiences do not match up with what we think the Bible has declared. These are troubling times in the life of people for these experiences challenge our faith and our view of God. This is the crisis of faith, when our faith is tested against the harsh times of confusion and the fear that we will not survive with our faith intact. This is the type of trial that will make us a better or a bitter person. It has been unfortunate that many people have been made bitter and angry at God and never recover. On the other hand, I have been encouraged by those struggling saints who have pushed through the darkness and developed a deeper maturity in God as the result of their trust in God.

In order for our anger to abate, it must be expressed or released. Jeremiah shows us a way he released his anger to God. He did not withhold it. He spoke to God and expressed his anger at what he believed was an unfair and disproportionate show of wrath upon the people.

Give yourself permission to be angry. It is only a sign of our humanity. God can handle us being angry at Him. He can deal with our anger. He allowed the psalmist to be concerned and express his agitation toward God. Our anger is an expression of our inner pain because of a great loss. God understands and remains deeply in love with us. Just a word of warning. Do not remain in your anger. Get it out. Get it over. If you do not, you will find yourself in a deep, dark place that is called depression.

When you release your anger in a productive way, it becomes a tool that helps you discover a different side of the character of God. You discover that He is patient with you. He gives you the confidence that He can be trusted. You then discover His peace is greater than your grief and loss in life. As you express your anger to God, you might find it very helpful to seek reconciliation with those who hurt you. Seek to live peacefully with all people as much as you can. Forgive quickly for this is helpful to your inner healing. The truth is that often we are angry with our deceased love one for leaving us. I do not think it weird to visit their grave and release them. Understand they left a hole in your soul, but it's fine that they are safe in the presence of God. Sometimes keeping a journal of your thoughts and feelings will help release the anger. Here, in your writings you can be honest and release the hurt. Reading the Psalms helps us to know that we have not been singled out by God to be "picked on." Many others have passed through the same struggles with anger and resentment. God is gracious to allow other people to come alongside of us to encourage us in the future victory over anger. A trusted friend is a resource greater than gold. They listen without judgment. They love without conditions. They might not fully understand, but they are present with you.

As you progress through the anger and the grief clouds begin to vanish, one day standing on the other side of the test you will say, "I never want to go through a test like that again, but I would not take anything for the journey." You will then rejoice with the psalmist, "I will sing to the Lord because He is good to me" (13:6, NLT). Chapter 2 has revealed a side of God's personality as well as the pain of Jeremiah. God's wrath has been on display as an instrument to punish rebellious Judah. Jeremiah was afforded a private look into his grieving heart for the people to whom he ministered.

Notes

1. Theophile J. Meek and William P. Merrill, Vol. 6, *The Interpreter's Bible* (Nashville: Abington Press, 1956), 16.

2. Walter C. Kaiser, *A Biblical Approach to Personal Suffering* (Eugene: Wipf & Stock Publishers, 1980), 73.

3. Ken Gire, *Windows of the Soul* (Grand Rapids: Zondervan Press, 1966), 195.

4. Caleb Colbey, "God's Anger." apologeticspress.org/article/1462.

5. J.I. Packer, *Knowing God* (Dowvers Grove: InterVarsity Press, 1973), 151-152.

6. Packer, Ibid., 156.

7. https://www.goodreads.com/quotes/71023-grow-old-along-with-me-the-best-is-yet-to.

8. F.B. Huey Jr., *The New American Commentary* (Nashville: Broadman Press, 1993), 461.

9. R.C. Sproul, "Does Prayer Change God's Mind?" www.ligonier.org/blog/does-prayer-change-gods-mind/.

10. Kaiser, *A Biblical Approach to Personal Suffering*, 43.

11. H. Norman Wright, *Experiencing Grief* (Nashville: B&H Publishing Corp., 2004), 43.

Chapter 3
Personality of Grief

The writing style of Jeremiah changes slightly in Chapter 3. He continues with the acrostic style but with a twist. Chapters 1, 2, 4 and 5 all have twenty-two verses with each verse beginning with the consecutive letters of the Hebrew alphabet. Chapter 3 has sixty-six verses (three times more than the other four chapters). Jeremiah sections these sixty-six verses into sets of threes. Each of the section of threes begins with consecutive letters of the Hebrew alphabet. The next three verses begin with the second letter of the alphabet and so on, until all twenty-two letters are used to begin the sixty-six verses.

One point of debate among many scholars centers around this central chapter of Lamentations. Was the writer expressing his personal sorrow and lament, or was the writer representing the nation? Personally, I lean toward the writer (Jeremiah) speaking of his personal pain and loss as he writes. My reason is found in the following verses: 1, 14, 27, 35, 39 and 53. The opposing view will suggest that Jeremiah writes and speaks for the nation. That view is supported by the change of pronouns from "I" to "we" (verses 20, 40-47). This seems to be a change in his style, but admittedly the decision is difficult to make as to for whom the writer is speaking. However, Jeremiah has expressed himself as he wrote in Chapter 2, verses 20-22, and I also think he speaks personally in Chapter 3. Examples of how the use of pronouns changes in each section will be highlighted as the Scripture unfolds. Either opinion expresses a deep heart felt pain because of so much loss in the lives of the people.

The breakdown of Chapter 3 is as follows: Verses 1-20 speak of the writer's distress, verses 21-39 speak of his delight, verses 40-51 speak of his despair, and verses 52-66 deal with his declaration.

Chapter 3, verses 1-20 is an expression of the writer's distress. Verse 1 sets the tone for the following 19 verses. He begins with the personal pronoun "I." Clearly, these words come from the heart of the great prophet. He has suffered personally from God's rod of judgment. Many of the expressions Jeremiah uses within this chapter offer great proof that he is the author of Lamentations (Jeremiah 20:7/Lamentations 3:14; Jeremiah 14:11-12/Lamentations 3:8; Jeremiah 37:16, 38:1-6, Jeremiah 7:16, 11:14, 14:11/Lamentations 3:8). The sufferings of Jeremiah made him feel with the people as he did in Chapter 2. His suffering was personal, and he personally identified with the hurting people of Judah.

This is the strength of a wise counselor. They are not disconnected from personal pain. They too have been wounded. They too have lost and grieved. God has allowed a sense of brokenness within their soul so that the counselor has at some point been counseled. He has been helped, and his ultimate desire is to help others reach their maximum life with less pain. Being wounded and recovered makes the greatest of sympathizers and healers.

The distress of Jeremiah is so great that he feels disconnected with God. This distance between God and him is revealed because Jeremiah does not mention God's name until verse 18.

Jeremiah proceeds to give many metaphors that describe his distress. He describes his distress as darkness (verse 2). This is his confession of confusion. He does not understand the purpose that God has for leading him into this dark place in his life. He knows that he is not in darkness by personal foolish choices, but that God has intentionally put him there in a place void of light. In the midst of the darkness, Jeremiah thinks that God has turned against him (verse 3). Wherever he turns, God is waiting to deliver more harshness upon him. This type of distress upon Jeremiah is readily seen in his physical body. His skin is becoming wrinkled because of stress. His body is breaking down. His stature is frail and his bones are broken because the heavy hand of judgment from God is upon him (verse 4).

Verse 5 reveals the distress in another metaphor. He describes his feelings as being like a city that is surrounded by the enemy. He is captured by anguish and fear. He sees himself being in a place where no exit signs are posted. There is no escape. There is no way out of this distress. He is trapped without hope. Worry, weariness, and grief fill his life. Jeremiah's sense of separation from God reaches its depth of expression in verse 6, which is a reference to Psalm 143:4. He describes his feeling as a dead man whose body has been placed in a dark grave. Jeremiah may mean that he feels like he is in hell, forever separated from God. He feels that he has died on the inside without any hope to live again. Perhaps Psalm 88, verses 5-7 and verse 12 best describes Jeremiah's distress as he feels as one who has died long ago only to be forgotten forever.

Jeremiah continues the theme of captivity in verses 7-9. In these verses he speaks as a prisoner held captive in a dungeon. Heavy chains forbid him freedom to move. He expresses what many grieving people feel when they think they cannot move from one stage of grief to the next. Jeremiah feels surrounded by high walls that are made of "hewn stones" (KJV). The use of the phrase "hewn stones" may mean that these stones were engineered on purpose and chosen especially for Jeremiah's prison. Jeremiah is very insightful to recognize God's involvement in his life and how He especially has designed the journey for his good and God's glory. Jeremiah feels like a prisoner in the situation. The first response of any one in captivity is to cry out for freedom. Jeremiah cries out for release, but God has blocked his prayers. Jeremiah experiences what many people do in the grieving moments of life; he feels the absence of God. Jeremiah feels that freedom is impossible because the walls that surround him are very high, and the road to freedom seems impossible.

Our first response, though, in those times of imprisonment by our inner pain or pressing circumstances is that we cry out for release. This response may not be the best, nor is it the most honoring to God. Many of our situations are "hewn" from God's hand for the purpose of more than our release. God seeks to teach us certain truths that we could never learn from times of ease and comfort. So, our first response should be to ask God, "What are You trying to teach me while I am in this circumstance that You have allowed to come into my life?"

There are times in a person's life when God will allow us to be placed in a prison of circumstances with no exits available. These are times that God has captured our full attention. No one totally understands the entire purposes of God. Generally speaking, God is at work developing a person for His purposes and for the individual's spiritual maturity. During these specific moments when God has us imprisoned, He teaches us those Christlike qualities of humility, obedience, patience, and faith. These traits of Christ are not taught in the textbooks of higher learning, but in the times of isolation when God teaches us by experience one on one.

Being captured by God affords us the honor of knowing Him in a more intimate way.

We connect with Him as Paul described in Philippians 3:10: "That I may know Him and the power of His resurrection, and the fellowship of His sufferings, being conformed to His death."

All true believers would boast to know of the power of God that raised Christ from the tomb. However, few want to participate with Christ and suffer the many ways Christ did. Even fewer desire to die physically or selfishly to our wills to experience resurrection power. Those who do are positioned at the feet of the Great Teacher to learn of Him. It is at the feet of our Lord that we are on holy ground.

If God has placed you into a dungeon of despair, obscurity, or self-death, it is actually a blessing. Therefore, do not think that God has abandoned you. He may be silent and still in your life, but He is preparing you to hear Him. He is getting you ready for future use. He is conditioning you for the race that He has set before you. Do not lose heart. Do not give in to fearful feelings. You are safe in His confinement. Paul reminds us of God's constant work as he writes: "Being confident of this very thing, that He who has begun a good work in you will complete it until the day of Jesus Christ" (Philippians 1:6).

Jeremiah sees himself as a hunted man who soon is to be torn apart by wild beasts waiting for the right time to pounce upon him (verses 1-3). Poor Jeremiah. His perspective of God is so twisted. To Jeremiah, God is the hunter, and he is the hunted. He is the victim standing helpless before God. God has bent His bow and aimed His arrow at the prophet (verse 13).

The imagery changes in verses 14 and 15. These verses can be applied to Jerusalem for they are the laughingstock of other nations. However, these verses also still can be applied to Jeremiah's personal suffering.[1] He is mocked and laughed at by the townspeople. His countrymen show no kindness. He is given no consolation in his personal humiliation.

Jeremiah reaches the pits of despair in verses 15-20. This is a painful picture of a person who is the recipient of some very harsh treatment from God. He feels that God has forced bitterness upon him. To Jeremiah, God has treated him with cruelness. He describes God as making him eat rocks and breaking out his teeth, and then grinding Jeremiah into ashes. (This is symbolism of the despair and sadness that accompanies grief). Jeremiah feels the pain of one who lacks inner peace. He has forgotten what it means to be prosperous because it has been so long since he has experienced such blessings.

This is a dark time for Jeremiah. His hope is gone from his heart. He no longer thinks God will rescue him from this despair. His inward pain is so great that he cannot focus on anything but negative thoughts. Ingrained within his mind is emotional trauma, and he is well on his way to despair and severe depression.

The emotional weight upon Jeremiah's spirit was of such heaviness that he expresses his grief in pictures of darkness, of a dungeon, and writhing death. These are bleak portraits of his inner spirit, and not one image is positive in his writing. Jeremiah is expressing his grief over his beloved city, and he is right to do so. In our search for healing from our grief, part of the process is to express it to someone verbally.

There is something healing in verbally expressing the inner pain. When you "name" the reason for the grief, it acts like a valve to release the hurt. Jeremiah often expressed his grief through tears as well as calling out to God in prayer. Earlier Jeremiah wrote of how God has given us these tear ducts for a purpose that expresses our words in liquid form. The ability of Jeremiah to cry is an advantage that many people, especially men, do not exercise. From childhood, men have been programmed "to be strong" and not cry. Therefore, when the heart of a man is broken, he feels it is beneath his male image to cry. However, to refrain from a display of tears in the midst of grief is not emotionally healthy. This may be one reason our female counterpart survives us by 4.8 years.[2] For those who read these words and say that "Christian faith is mocked when people cry," I must respond by saying that just because one is faithful to Christ does not cancel our personal feelings.

There is no biblical support for the philosophy of stoicism. Stoicism is a teaching that flourished in the Roman and Greek world that taught that an individual should be free from feelings of pain or grief. God made us with the ability to show faith and feelings at the same time. Christ taught us this truth by His example that it is quite permissible to show inner pain in tears. Therefore, as one expresses inner grief through tears, he will find a wonderful natural relief that is emotionally healthy.

Within this section of Jeremiah's inward portrait, he expresses the feeling of "God forsakenness." This inner feeling is true of many grieving people, and it is one of the many mile markers on the journey of wellbeing. This feeling can be further described as thinking that God is no longer with you in the pain. Aloneness, betrayal, and isolation are a part of this darkness. Jeremiah feels trapped in a deep prison with no signs of release or exit. He feels all the emotions of a man in deep grief and sorrow.

To a large degree, I have lived in that darkness as did Jeremiah. I can quickly echo the statements of the prophet. I write not from the ivory castle of serenity but from the dungeon of darkness, and there is no darkness like the inner feeling of being forsaken by God. I remember so clearly the dark thoughts that hung over my head like a black cloud that would not go away. There were feelings of failure as a pastor because the attendance was not as great as I expected it to be, and there were more people becoming my enemies than my co-laborers. How could this be when I faithfully preached and lived the truth? Why would God not bless my ministry? I surmised that God had turned against me perhaps for some sin of long ago. Even though I had confessed and repented from all my known sin, perhaps God chose to punish me by not blessing my ministry. My desire since youth was to be used of God, but it seemed that God deemed me unusable.

I began to think that I had simply wasted my life. I spent years in study and training to be prepared for God to use me, only to come to this dead end of a prison of uselessness and hopelessness. Satan was so quick to inform me that the life I lived for Christ was a total waste.

Hopelessness is the friend of forsakenness. I have read somewhere that people can live more than three weeks without food, about one week without water, and only three minutes without oxygen. These are the basic necessities of life. How long can a person live without hope? I do not know, but my guess is not long at all. Just as food, water and oxygen are the basic necessities for physical life, so is hope to the spirit of a person. In the mind of a person without hope, death can become a welcomed friend. Death is the escape from a prison of hopelessness.

Another companion of the feeling of forsakenness is that it seems that God has turned a deaf ear to our prayers. Every prayer seems to be met with silence. One can feel the heavy sense of forsakenness as God Himself refuses to give attention to our desperate cries for release from the darkness. I understand what Jeremiah felt as he said, "Surely He has turned His hand against me time and time again throughout the day" (3:3). My mind raced to those verses in Scripture that promise God will not leave us, and that God will answer our prayers when His conditions are met, and that the prayer of a righteous man avails much, but my experience did not match up with those promises at that time. This, indeed, was a time of darkness for me.

I began to realize some of the human feelings of Christ as He prayed on the cross, "My God, My God, why have You forsaken me?" (Mark 15:34). I realized that Christ in all of His sinless perfection felt the pain of being forsaken of God more intense than I in my broken condition. Nevertheless, for me, the feeling of aloneness that God allowed me to feel was very hurtful and certainly unforgettable.

Many of these inner feelings are accompanied by fear. Fear of the unknown. Fear of not understanding the "why" for God allowing you to experience these horrible emotions when you are clueless of the reasons for these catastrophes. There is suffering and grief, and on the surface it seems there is no purpose for the pain. Jeremiah and Job are co-sufferers. This period of grief seems to be only a waste of time for it gives no true addition to life. Jeremiah, like many people today, see no value to the grief in the moment. The epicenter of the grief is so hurtful that the focus is on the grief rather than the future benefits of the pain. All Jeremiah senses is that he has been left alone by God and isolated within the grief of his fallen city.

Only people who have traveled the grief journey can identify with Jeremiah. Those who sit in protective bubbles isolated from grief only read of these feelings that others have experienced, but cannot truly empathize with them.

James Dobson writes of one such pastor/writer named R.T. Kendall, who has traveled the same road as Jeremiah. R.T. Kendall was the senior minister of Westminster Chapel in London. Dr. Kendall is credited with the phrase of "the betrayal barrier." According to R.T. Kendall, the phrase describes a period of time when God seems to let His people down. This can occur at any time in the believers walk with God. This is what happened to Jeremiah after he had served God so faithfully since his youth by standing for God in difficult times and faithfully proclaiming God's word. God appears to have left Jeremiah as a lonely man in a dungeon and as a forgotten dead man in the grave. The honest human response to God is, "If this is the way you treat your faithful child, I want no more company with you, or if this is what you call love then no thanks." Kendall calls this a "tragic misunderstanding."[3]

Jeremiah is the example of one who potentially thinks God has lured him into service only to have left him in the midst of the struggle. Grief makes us feel forsaken by God if we do not understand that God loves us and has a purpose in all He allows us to experience. Since our finite brains cannot grasp the lofty wisdom of God, we can only offer invalid suggestions as to the reasoning of God. Sometimes there is just no human understanding to the ways of God (Isaiah 55:8-9). The only way Jeremiah could, or we can, find a lifeboat in the sea of grief is to trust in an all-wise God who is in full control of our lives and is deeply in love with us. This is one way to respond positively to the feelings of forsakenness during our grief. This trust placed in God is one way to respond positively to the feelings of forsakenness during grief.

There is another element in the emotions of Jeremiah that is evident in these verses. Jeremiah grieves deeply for his people and country because of their great loss. One of the many telling signs of grief is depression. Whenever there is a loss of something or someone in our lives, grief and depression soon will follow.

Jeremiah describes his journey of grief in vivid images. Behind the grief lurks the pain of depression. He speaks of darkness without light (verse 2). He believes God is against him at all times (verse 3). He is filled with distress (verse 5). He thinks God no longer listens to him or that God does not care about his plight (verse 8). He feels surrounded — trapped by high walls that show no exits for his escape (verse 9). He thinks God is hunting him down for his destruction (verse 10). He thinks people are against him (verse 14). To Jeremiah, God has made his life bitter and taken away the peace, joy, hope, and splendor of life (verses 15, 17, 18).

Grief has the potential to make us feel that everyone, including God, is our enemy. Depression makes us entertain thoughts that we would never think apart from mental pain. When a grieving person sees life through his loss and begins to think that the one person (God) who promised never to leave him and to always be sufficient for his needs has left him and does not care, the result is depression.

The purpose of this writing is not to go into great detail concerning depression. However, the reader must be aware that to have feelings of melancholy after a loss is natural and a sign that one is working through the grief process in a healthy manner.[4] There is a problem when the grieving person gets hung up in the depression for a period of time.

Dr. Nancy Donovan, an instructor at Harvard Medical School, says, "If you are experiencing mood or cognitive changes that last for more than a few weeks, it's a good idea to bring this up with your doctor or consult a mental health specialist to help sort out possible causes."[5]

Personally, I wish I had followed the advice of the good doctor. I struggled with depression almost two years before seeking the help of a Bible-based counselor. I had taken the medication prescribed by my doctor, but I needed something more than a covering up of the inner pain. I needed a way out of the prison of hopeless despair. I needed someone to help me get free from the clutch of an inner hell that no matter what I did to help myself I found no freedom.

I woke suddenly at 1 a.m. I put my feet firmly on the floor as I sat on the side of my bed. To me, it was a wake-up call from God with a clear message to my heart that said, "Go see a counselor." I began early that day looking for a counselor and found one who spoke of his desire to help and his love for pastors. I intentionally selected a counselor a great distance from the church I served. In my mindset, I did not want anyone to know that I needed help for my depression. My pride would not allow me to admit I needed help. I thought I could eventually work out a plan for overcoming my depression. In my way of thinking, counseling was for weak-minded people who were not strong or disciplined enough to work through their emotions. Therefore, I would never have pictured me on a counselor's couch.

April 12, 2011 is a date that I will not easily forget. On that date I remember driving my car into the hospital parking lot of Palmetto Baptist Hospital in Columbia, S.C. I remember entering the area of the hospital that was designated as "Mental Health." My heart sank in my being as I said, "Dear God, why are you allowing me to be so dehumanized by this experience?" I felt stripped of all dignity and self-esteem. Seeing that sign upon the hospital wall was what seemed to be the final blow to my personhood. I felt as though so much of my life was just ripped from my chest. Regardless of all the thoughts that ran through my mind, I must admit that sign gave me a new sense of reality. I had to admit that I was not well mentally and that a part of my life was out of balance. That truth put my life into a new perspective that I had never before experienced. Now, instead of me ministering to others, I became the one who needed to be ministered to. I went to the hospital not to visit with someone sick, but because I was the sick one. I felt so embarrassed and ashamed of my status of being in need of help from the mental health unit of the hospital. However, I was not mentally healthy, and I did need to be there.

The counselor was very helpful and sympathetic. After explaining my mental state, I was given a test to determine the seriousness of my depressed state. The counselor graded the test and said my score showed that the level of depression was very high. He went on to say, "In all my years of dealing with depressed individuals, no one has ever scored this level." Then came the verdict. "You are functional. You are not bi-polar. You are clinically depressed, but I can help," he said.

I was asked to describe what I felt about my depression. I remember saying, "It is a very dark hole wherein I am held as a prisoner. There is no hope. There is no light. There are no exit signs to point the way out of the darkness." At the end of the session, I was given the counselor's private phone number. He made me promise that I would not hurt myself, and if I thought of doing so that I would call him immediately. After the counseling session, he led me out of a different door to exit the building (to preserve my privacy).

In that state of depression, I have come to believe that a person can be dead while he is alive. There can be a heartbeat and a warm body, but the life may be gone from it. My eyes told the story of my lifeless spirit. It has been said that the eye is the window of the soul, and if that be true, I was dead yet alive. My wife said she could look into my eyes and could see only darkness. That was my state. I have also concluded that you do not have to die to be in hell, to be in a wretched, lonely, painful condition. Of course, this is not the hell that is described in the Bible, but while alive I lived in some of the torments. In my case, depression brought with it a wretchedness, darkness, loneliness, and separation from humanity and God, and a feeling of inward pain that is a part of the literal hell described in the Scriptures. Another thought came to me during the most severe times of my depression that I had never before experienced. As a minster I have had the unfortunate experience of conducting the services of someone who had committed suicide. I often wondered how a person could take such extreme measures as to take his own life. After experiencing the most painful times of my journey, I now think I have a little insight as to why someone would take this opinion in life.

The depressed person is in such deep emotional pain. The pain is as real as a gaping wound to the physical body. Even though you cannot see the emotional cut, it is there, it is real, and it is painful. Sometimes the pain is so extreme that the suffering person does not fear death. In fact, it may be seen as a relief. There is such a loss of hope that giving up life becomes an option to escape the dark place. To the person who is depressed, words sometimes cannot fully express the pain or sadness within. Those who are not given to depression often do not understand their loved ones' inner trauma.

They use phrases such as: come on and pick yourself up by the bootstraps and get on with your life, or cheer up, life is great, or you have no reason to be depressed. These types of phrases, although used by people who mean well, do not help the victim of depression rise above the pain. One might as well tell an amputee to grow another limb. It is very difficult to fully understand depression unless you have been in its grip. Therefore, feeling as though no one can relate or understand his cry for help, the individual turns to suicide as an extreme way to show people their severe pain rather than explaining their pain. This is one reason a trained counselor is very important to the depressed person. The counselor can honestly understand, show deep concern, and help the depressed one find a better route to recovery.

The second section of Chapter 3 of Lamentations brings us to verses 21-39. This is a paragraph of delight. Without question these verses are a wonderful transition in the attitude of Jeremiah. Especially true is that these verses are some of the most encouraging and hopeful in this book, and, in this writer's opinion, some of the most beautiful in all the Old Testament. Jeremiah, who has described his condition as one who is forgotten and hopeless, now finds himself at the apex of faithfulness. He offers praise upon praise to our God of love, compassion, fairness, and justice. During this time, Jeremiah lifts his eyes off of the destruction of the city and places them on the Lord. This is a wonderful doxology as Jeremiah worships God with praise and adoration. It is easy to get caught up in Jeremiah's delight of our Lord.

Out of the pit of despair, Jeremiah rises to the heights of delight. His mood changes from desperation to hope. He once saw God as seeking him out for destruction. Now, Jeremiah sees God as faithful and loyal to His people (verses 21-24). Jeremiah is experiencing a change of mind. He admits his thought process was wrong and the result was a negative view of God. In the midst of his depressed mind, his thoughts had become not only negative but narrow as he thought of God. He saw his pitiful situation as hopeless. He saw God as harsh and vindictive. His inner pain made him forget the goodness and grace of God for His people.

Jeremiah puts his finger upon a very important part of our mind and how it reacts to grief. Grief brings along with it many emotions. These emotions can include anger, guilt, denial, and acceptance. Every day offers a different emotion that one can choose. I purposefully use the word "choose" because the grieving person does have the power to decide how he or she will respond to grief. Sometimes there are two thoughts competing for the most attention for that day. One of the many keys that unlock our understanding of the grief process is to realize that we are given choices as to how we respond to grief.

You and I can choose to react to grief. We can believe this grief is so great that we are trapped and left without hope. We can become angry at God for allowing the loss in life. We can think of ourselves as a helpless victim. We can form untrue opinions about God's character by accusing Him of being unloving, unkind, and unfair. Our foolish pride can cause us to elevate ourselves to an equal level with God, so that we think we can look God in the eye and argue with His decision to permit this grief in our lives. We can become bitter and blame others for our loss in life. If it is a mate, we might blame the doctor for not doing enough to help. We might blame ourselves for not giving enough attention to our mate's symptoms of sickness. When our relationships fail, and we lose the love of a companion, we might blame him or her. We can become an isolationist and never trust people again. For example, if we lose our job, we believe the co-worker or the supervisor or someone else was always out to get us. There is no end to how we can respond to our grief.

Another way, the mature way, is to act in the onslaught of grief. This means that we must face our grief with the truth that is given to us in God's word. We become proactive in dealing with our grief. Only when we cut through the shallow emotions and lay a firm grip upon the truth can we move forward in the grief process that leads to our eventual healing. As we act to find healing in grief, we examine our thoughts and in time have to release them because they are not healthy. Emotions must be examined to see if they can be trusted. Acting to get past the pain means talking about what you are thinking to someone who is a confidant and who can help you evaluate your emotions. Here is the release valve that lets off the internal pressure. Lastly, you need some alone time whereby God has you only to Himself, and He feeds your mind with His truth, love, and grace. He is the real healer. Jesus himself demonstrated the importance of time alone with the Father. There is no better source where our inner spirit can be refreshed.

Once you have decided to act in ways that are beneficial and will help you advance through the grief process, you must decide what must be done. It is of utmost importance to understand that your mind is the tool that can change your attitude. Jeremiah understood this in verse 21. One discovers that his attitude turned from despair to hope. Grief is diminished from a person's heart as the mind focuses upon the character of God.

The Bible is laced with passages that deal with the power of the thought life. Paul wrote in Philippians 4:8:

> *Finally, brethren, whatever things are true, whatever things are noble, whatever things are just, whatever things are pure, whatever things are lovely, whatever things are of good report, if there is any virtue and if there is anything praiseworthy — meditate on these things.*

In the world of information technology, there is a phrase that can help us understand the meaning of this verse: "Garbage in — Garbage out." The programmer feeds the computer poor information, and it comes out as poor information. The reverse is true in the spiritual world. Positive thoughts and valuable and encouraging words going into the mind will yield a great defense against the negativity which hinders a positive attitude.

Paul wrote in Romans 12:2: "And be not conformed to this world:

but be ye transformed by the renewing of your mind, that ye may prove what is that good, and acceptable, and perfect will of God" (KJV).

Paul emphasized that Christians do not have to be imitators of the world. Therefore, Christians do not have to allow grief to enslave them like many non-Christians do. The way to escape the grip of grief is to transform your mind. One must take the initiative to allow the Holy Spirit to constantly work in his mind. We have the responsibility to become involved. We cannot be passive if we are to move through grief. When the Holy Spirit changes our inner person (heart), He does so in a way that is both pleasing to God and helpful to us.

Solomon, out of God's wisdom, spoke to the issue of the thought life in Proverbs 23:7 when he said: "For as [a man] thinks in his heart, so is he."

Henry Ford once said, "Whether you think you can or you think you can't … you're right."

The simple truth is, what you put into your mind, you will retrieve by the aid of the Holy Spirit to assist you in overcoming grief.

Here are only a few selected Scripture references to fill your mind with the truth of God. These verses are special to me, and I list the references along with personal thoughts in hopes that God will use them to heal your hurting heart.

- John 14:18: God's spirit in me is a constant companion.
- John 14:27: God gives me His peace so my heart need not be troubled.
- Philippians 1:6: God has not finished His work in me. The process of His work is often painful, but the result is most wonderful.
- Philippians 3:13: There are some things in life that I need to release (e.g., toxic relationships, revenge, unforgiveness, self-imposed guilt). There are some things I need to reach for

(i.e., a deeper relationship with Christ).

- Philippians 4:13: God will give me strength to pass through the darkness.
- Philippians 4:19: God will meet my need of any kind (i.e., grief from a loss). The greatness of His riches in Christ, His vault of blessings to meet my emotional, physical, spiritual needs is greater than I can imagine.
- Peter 1:6: "For a season" means my problems are given a limitation. They will not be upon me forever. My grief has an expiration date.
- Peter 1:3: God in Christ already has given to me all that I will ever need in this life to be godly. My Father met my needs before I even knew I had any needs.
- Romans 8:28: All of my moments and experiences that are darkened by defeat and sorrow mixed in with moments of praise and celebration become the recipe that produces good for me and glory for Christ. He has a plan that I might not understand, but I trust Him with the results.
- Jeremiah 29:11: God in His wisdom has me on a course of His own desire. I cooperate with Him as I obey. I do not have to agree or know of His plan. My obligation is to trust. I rarely know why God allows me to pass through the gauntlet of sorrow. He has a larger view in sight than I do. I just trust and obey.
- Joshua 1:9: I have no need to fear any person or event. God is with me.
- Psalm 23: The Lord is my shepherd, and He meets my needs.
- Psalm 46:1: God is our refuge and strength.
- Psalm 55:22: The Lord sustains us. We can trust Him with our burdens.
- Isaiah 43:2: In every extreme I might face, God protects me as

long as I am walking in His way.

- Isaiah 49:16: God has my name written on the palms (plural) of His hands (plural). He will never forget me.
- Isaiah 54:7: "For a mere moment I have forsaken you, but with great mercies I will gather you."

As I alluded to previously, my favorite is Joel 2:25: God will restore all that has been taken. He might do His act of restoration on earth, or He may not. However, He will restore all in heaven. My heart broken in grief will be restored. My losses on earth will be restored when I see my friends in heaven. God be blessed.

The mind is such a powerful tool, and it helps us refocus and reprogram our thoughts about our grief and God. We must remember that Satan will attack the mind with intense aggression. In Ephesians 6:17, Paul instructs the church to put on the helmet of salvation as a vital part of the preparation for spiritual warfare. The helmet is for the protection of the head in case of satanic assault in the mind and thought system of the Christian. Without question, Paul is wise to offer this instruction because the mind is the battlefield in this epic fight. Paul knew the thought life of the child of God must be guarded with every effort. Satan's most vicious attack will begin and continue in our minds.

Satan's most effective tool is deception. He is the father of all lies (John 8:44). His arrows of deception take many forms that cause havoc in the mind of the believer who has not armed himself with the truth of God's word. Lies, doubt, fear, baseless thoughts of loss of security, and suffering are his choice weapons toward the person laden with grief. Satan suggests to the one heavy in heart that God has abandoned him to suffer alone. He makes his lies so real as he continuously says, "God does not love you. If He did, He would not have allowed your loved one to die." Often, he lies by using your experiences of guilt for not doing enough to prevent a loss and then reinforces the guilt by using blame and a poor self-image that declares that you are at fault. Satan is heartless, and he takes no prisoners in the battle for your mind. He is relentless in his brutal attack against the truth.

How can this battle of your thoughts be won? There is only one way. The knowledge of God's truth is the weapon for every struggling person. The truth alone is not strong enough to overcome Satan's attack. You must know the truth and then apply the truth of God's word when Satan brings a lie to your mind. There is nothing more powerful than God's truth in dealing with Satan's falsehoods, as you incorporate God's truth in your mind. It is light that overcomes the darkness. God's truth allows us to recognize Satan's deception and gives us victory over his lies. Sometimes it takes a trained counselor to help us through the deception. We are so consumed by the grief and Satan's deception that we cannot understand clearly how to find our way into the light of truth.

Jeremiah stated the following in verse 21: "This I recall (remembered) to my mind, therefore have I hope." Here is a wonderful example of how the truth of God operating against the lies of hopelessness in Jeremiah's mind was stronger than deception. However, Jeremiah had to think. He took action, and although his eyes saw hopelessness around him, he knew God supplies hope in hard times. What God had previously told him concerning hope, he remembered in the midst of grief.

Verses 22-25 give forth the reasons for the hope. He begins by thinking of the wonderful action of God's *hesed* (loving-kindness) that reaches out to those who are deep in despair. Just when Jeremiah is at his lowest moment, God covers him with mercy and gives him hope. God proves Himself to be merciful and shows His character to be sufficient to meet the needs of His grieving prophet. Jeremiah closes this paragraph of praise to God by sounding forth in verse 24: "I say to myself, 'The Lord is my portion; therefore I will wait for him'" (NIV).

This particular verse is filled with many truths that those who grieve must apply to their lives. Once again, the truth of our personal involvement in dealing with grief is expressed. The phrase "I say to myself" is important for it reinforces the truth that sometimes I have to make a decision to do my part to rise beyond this consuming grief. The psalmist in Chapter 42, verse 5 gives an excellent example of this. He speaks to himself for the purpose of correcting his direction away from depression. He asks, "Why are you cast down, O my soul? And why are you disquieted within me? Hope in God: for I shall yet praise Him for the help of His countenance."

The wonderful truth is that God will help us to navigate through the anguish in our soul. Trained godly counselors help us to voice our feelings, and physicians can prescribe medications that can correct chemical imbalances in our brains, but God has so designed us that we, too, must be a part of the healing process. The psalmist as well as Jeremiah reveals the part that we play in the process of our healing. We must decide to get better. We have to speak truth to ourselves from the Scripture. We must make the internal choice that determines our moving forward in the grief process.

Jeremiah writes two of the most encouraging verses in Chapter 3, verses 22 and 23: "Through the Lord's mercies we are not consumed, because His compassions fail not. They are new every morning; great is Your faithfulness."

These verses ring with a resounding hope in the character of God that shows His compassion, love, mercy, and concern for us every day. Every morning God gives to our grieving hearts sufficient mercy that allows us strength for that day. What a wonderful thought that our heavenly father is faithful and kind to us who are caught in the grip of grief.

God has allowed Jeremiah to experience the ravages of deep prolonged grief for our example. Perhaps God records this so we might have the assurance that we, like Jeremiah, can find hope in God.

Verse 24 spawns another truth as it concerns the promise of God to Israel. This verse is a reference to Numbers 18:20. The subject is the land of Canaan as the inheritance of Israel. However, the land is now possessed by foreign occupiers. God allowed every foundation of Judah's society to be crushed. The families, the riches and the temple all were destroyed. Yet the prophet believes in spite of all their losses that God is their ultimate inheritance. Therefore, it is very helpful in seasons of grief to remind ourselves that our hope is not in those things we have lost, but our hope is in who we have: our faithful God whose mercies toward us are fresh every morning.

I am convinced that some of the greatest blessings are not always what is given to us, but rather what is taken from us. When we become so consumed by temporary items that we lose focus upon God, we have an idolatrous lifestyle. God's greatest desire is for us to position Him as the priority of our lives. He will not allow for any rivals as is demonstrated in the writings of Jeremiah and the Ten Commandments (Exodus 23:3). There are times when possessions have replaced God from His rightful position of first place in our lives. When Christians allow things to be priorities over God, they invite unhappiness and confusion in their lives. The truth is that God demands the priority in our lives (Exodus 20:3; Mark 12:30; Matthew 6:33). When Christians give Christ first place, then they eventually will grow to understand that loss is a blessing in disguise. The ultimate desire of God for your life is met when He is the priority of your life. Scripture teaches that God is the rock of our lives. He is the only thing that is not temporal. He is eternal in nature. Because of God's wonderful character, Jeremiah says he has hope in God. God has proven Himself to be loving, compassionate, and faithful to His word; therefore, Jeremiah sees these qualities as his foundation for hope. God is Jeremiah's patron or "inheritance," and that is sufficient for Jeremiah.

Verses 25-39 feature the theme of the goodness of God. The word "good" is found in verses 25, 26, and 27. God is defined as "practical or material good, abstract goodness such as beauty and moral good."[6] Jeremiah offers the idea that God is good to those who are patient and wait upon Him (verse 25). When a person hopes in God and waits upon God for help (verse 26), they have the assurance that they, like Jeremiah, can find hope in God even in the depth of their grief.

God is good to those who "wait" for Him (verse 25a). When someone grieves, yet expresses confident hope in God, he is able to wait patiently upon God to do His work in his life. He has learned patience in his time of grief. This is an Old Testament truth that is developed more in the New Testament. Paul spoke of the advantages of patience in Romans 5:3-5. It is such a comforting thought to know that God always has a purpose in our grief. When God permits these times of loss and grief, it is never without an objective. You may not recognize His purpose at the origin of grief, but as you remain faithful to Him, in due time He often makes us aware of His purpose. This is especially true in the life of the child of God. During the grieving, you discover a new essence of God's goodness as you wait upon Him and seek Him. The person who hopes in God as they wait upon Him to accomplish His purpose for grief will find God to be good.

Perhaps a definition for the word "wait" is necessary at this juncture. To wait on God does not mean to be idle. It does not mean for us to sit still and do nothing in our time of grief. We are to be active in prayerful seeking after God (verse 25b), asking Him for wisdom and insight and for ways we can honor Him in our grief. We ask Him for inner strength to withstand the doubts about God's character that Satan will hurl our way. We wait patiently upon God as we spend time in Scripture. We can find examples of many who grieved and discovered a positive disposition as they passed through the pain. Job, Naomi, and Elijah are a few for us to examine who demonstrate this response to grief. As you search the Scriptures and pray, God gives His faithful love and encouragement. He may show you the value of your grief. You may have discovered new ways for God to use you to help others in their grief (2 Corinthians 1:4-6). God's goodness is discovered as you wait on Him.

Verse 27 teaches us that the grieving person inherits good when they are stricken with a difficulty as a youth. This is a description of one who has learned early the pain that life can render. They have learned the pull and pressure of the yoke of God's way in their life. Those who suffer early in life learn to accept and adjust to God's purpose. The idea is, as a young person submits to God's work, he will be able to deal with weightier problems as he gets older. That type of submission brings a great maturity in a person's life.

It has been my privilege to know many people who from their youth carry a grievous weight of physical disabilities. As life for them has passed from youth to adulthood, they seem to have a mature attitude about what is important in life and what is not. Those in wheelchairs and on crutches do not fret over whether their shoes match their clothes or if they drive the most fashionable automobile. They are just content to be alive and able to enjoy mobility in life. They have weeded out the unnecessary things of life and are mature enough to discern the things of importance. Contentment is great gain to a person in grief who has discovered the important things in life. Grief has a way to mature us and streamline life.

The wisdom we glean from verses 28-30 is gathered from a group of three truths. Within these wonderful exhortations is the graduation in levels of intensity of grief. Verse 28 informs us that we often suffer in privacy. We find ourselves alone as we bear the grief. In reality, believers are never alone because God has promised His constant presence. The idea behind the verse is that we grieve without the presence of anyone else. In the privacy of our heart, we often carry a heavy burden of inner pain that no one knows about. We do not broadcast the pain and choose to suffer in silence. This is not all bad. God often pulls us away from others so He can have us only to Himself as He teaches us to be dependent upon Him for help and healing.

There is another level of intensity in our grief. This is the level of bearing our yoke in verse 29. To put one's mouth in the dust is an expression that is unique only to this book. The phrase is an ancient way of acknowledging complete submission to another person.[7] God has many ways to break a person's will without breaking his spirit. Grief and suffering are two of His choice instruments. He breaks us for His good purpose so that we are made conformable to the image of His son (Romans 8:29). I have often observed the people God uses greatly. They have a common trait: They have been wounded deeply in life, yet they did not get angry at God, but rather submitted their lives to His will. This is one of the greatest results of grief. When we submit to God, He uses us in spite of our wound.

Notice this level of increase in grief. In verse 28, the suffering is done in secret and in isolation. In verse 29, the suffering person is to submit to another. In verse 30, the pain is increased because there is physical humiliation. Submission to humiliation can only be done by faith in a God who is trustworthy to bring justice and who will make all things just in his time. It often is humiliating to have to go to a counselor for help through the grief process. I know. I have been there. However, it is comforting to know that God is in control of all things, even our moments of humiliation.

Verses 31-33 deal with an issue that is common during the grief process. The enemy, who is Satan, has a tactic that is quite successful. He plants within our hurting soul the thought that God has abandoned us. To reinforce this lie, he adds the thought that God does not care for us and does not love us. When our heart hurts and our thought life is not thoroughly strengthened with truth, we become easy prey for Satan's lies. Jeremiah gives us this wonderful truth that God has not forgotten about us, and His love and compassion are available to us in the grief process. God does not willingly attack us with affliction; His nature is that of unfailing love. These verses do not rule out the possibility that God does forsake His children for a brief period of time (Isaiah 53:7-8), and He does chastise His people (Hebrews 12:6), but those events are for the purpose of getting our focus upon Him and to correct us from a wrong direction in life. However, when God allows feelings of forsakenness and corrective discipline, He does so with brevity and purpose.

How comforting to hear truth from God rather than deception from Satan. When a person knows that God will not forsake them forever and that He loves them unconditionally, they tend to gain hope that in time the grief will pass and that God has not forgotten them. There is great confidence in God's good plan to carry us through the inner pain for a purpose that is honoring to Him. Our God cares. He is full of compassion. Just as grace is greater than any of our sin so God's compassion is greater than any of our grief. God does not have a flaw in His holy character that will allow Him to willfully pursue someone just to send affliction. He graciously loves people too much to allow these personal attacks that bring grief.

As I write these words about the grief experience today, a message from my wife informed me of some most unwanted and expected news concerning our youngest daughter. Dedra and her husband Dillon were expecting their first child. She and Dillon went to the ob-gyn doctor for a second time to hear the baby's heartbeat. After the examination the doctor asked the anticipating couple to come into her office. It was there that the news that no parent wants to hear, "Mrs. Sain, we cannot find the baby's heartbeat." A picture of the well-formed baby was produced, and everything looked normal, but the baby had no heartbeat.

My dreams of being a grandfather to this child were destroyed. My hopes and goals for that baby were being played out in my mind already. Immediate grief was the heavy consequence of this great loss in my life. I will not begin to try to express what was in the hearts of Dillon and Dedra.

God showed me several things as I began to process this hurtful experience. He allowed me to review my personal journey from those earlier experiences of loss and grief and compare my reaction then to my most recent grief experience. Earlier experiences of grief brought on reactions such as anger at people, anger at God, hurt that focused inward, disillusionment with God's character and work in my life and in the world. Inside of me was a churning of all sorts of bad reactions that ultimately led to clinical depression. Today's news was met with a considerable volume of difference. As a grandfather, I hurt, for there is one grandchild I'll never hold or play with. I will never see his/her smile at birthday parties or at Christmas as he/she receives gifts. I will not be afforded the privilege to wear blue or pink at the reveal party. As a dad, I hurt for my son-in-law and daughter. I could not do anything to assuage the pain they experienced. I felt so helpless because I could not repair their broken hearts and dreams. I felt sorry for the great-grandparents of baby Sain. Being well into their years, they had hoped to see their great-grandchild come into the world.

I cried because of sadness. I cried because of joy. This time my pain was real and deeply felt, but my reaction to the grief was very different from earlier experiences. I cried out of joy. I was not angry with God.

In fact, through prayer I expressed to Him my faith in His wisdom as well as my lack of understanding of His ways. I expressed my complete confidence in His love for the entire family and trusted in Him to bring glory to Himself from this experience. Within my heart was absolutely no thought of God being unfair or unkind. I was at peace inside of my heart that God knows best, and I have full confidence in the ultimate purpose and plans for Dillon and Dedra. Rest, confidence, peace, and joy were the emotions in my heart. God allowed me to see the differences in my past responses from my present response. The difference is monumental and light years in their span. I can attribute this change to one thing: the grace of God. Yes, God used others to help, but the Great Physician has done a wonderful work of healing in my mind and heart. I do not claim that the healing is complete. I am still under construction, but to see where I was to where I am now is a picture of the wonderful grace of God working in me to bring a new awareness of His character and power to heal the broken heart of a person. I do not think my journey is over. There will be more times in my life that grief will come, but with the grace of God, He will give me the strength to pass through the pain and grow in Christ at every challenge.

Earlier experiences of loss only brought darkness and finality. However, this time God gave me a well-spring of eternal hope. I did not lose perspective in this tragic experience. I kept my eyes on a faithful, perfect, sufficient God. There were no feelings of being treated unfairly, and there was no anger. Rather, there was only quiet resolve that God has this experience under control. I knew God would heal my daughter and son-in-law's heart. I knew God had a greater purpose and plan than any I could ever conceive. I simply put my trust in God who is unfailing toward His children.

To say that I did not grieve the loss of a grandchild would be untrue. I did not find comfort in the trite comments, "Oh! It really was not a baby at just nine weeks." Yes, it was a baby. The baby is my fifth grandchild. Or, "Cheer up. You just try again for you are still young." These clichés are thoughtless and at best insensitive to grieving parents or grandparents. To lose a baby by miscarriage is more serious than striking out at bat during a baseball game. Yes, you might get another chance to hit, but to lose a baby is the loss of a human who had great potential in life. The grief of such a loss is real, and phrases will not help heal. In fact, those types of phrases can only add to the pain of loss for they dehumanize the child. What I did find solace in was just being confident in God's wisdom. I found peace by being with Dedra and Dillon. I found purpose in doing what I could do for them in their time of need. My heart found a very quiet inner peace by being able to move forward in the grief. I know that I have five grandchildren — four on earth and one in heaven. I know that one day when I get to heaven some boy or girl will run up to me and say, "Hey, Pa, I am the grandchild you never held. I never got to play with my cousins, but I have had a great time here just waiting on the rest of my family."

I have chosen to honor my fifth grandchild at Christmas by having a half pink and half blue stocking made to hang under the mantle along with the other four. That stocking will receive the same amount of money the other four will get. The difference is that colored stocking will donate its Christmas money to some charity of my choice. In this way, I will show my love and respect to baby Sain. I will not let baby Sain's memory die. I will celebrate the life that could have been and the child that I will one day see.

People grieve at their own pace. The healing from tragic loss might come quickly or at the pace of a sloth, but rising from the darkness of grief takes time. Although as I examine my reaction of grief from years ago to the last tragic loss of a grandchild, I must say that without the grace of God healing me and being my Great Physician, I probably would never have come as far as I have. The grace of God who exercises the healing salve over our broken soul, the wisdom of a godly counselor, and the element of time have combined their skills to give me some degree of healing. For these three elements in my life, I am eternally grateful.

On December 1, 2017, I received a phone call from my daughter, Dedra. I could tell she was crying. Her voice was quivering and barely audible through her tears. I tried to remain calm as I listened carefully as she spoke. I had to ask her to repeat herself once or twice because she was upset. I asked her where she was because I thought I would have to go to her. Then she told me the unexpected news that Danielle, our oldest daughter who was sixteen weeks pregnant, had been to the doctor for a scheduled exam and that her baby had died. The child was a little boy and would be delivered stillborn in two days.

I was shocked and surprised. I had seen Danielle's "baby bump" just days earlier. All seemed to be fine, and then as a bolt of lightning from the sky the news came that no grandfather wants to hear. There in heaven is another grandchild that I will have to wait to see, hold, and talk to.

My response was not anger or blame toward anyone, including God. I thought of Danielle and Adam, her husband. I thought of how her daddy should be there to console her, but the distance separates us for now. I thought of how she must feel inside, and how she and Adam must hurt as their dream for a third child fades away. I am praying that she does not feel guilty or punished for something she is completely innocent of. I am hoping that she will not become depressed as a result of her loss.

As soon as I heard, I called her. I asked her of her state of mind. She told me that she does not feel alone. She stated her confidence in God's love for her and His plan. Although she and Adam do not clearly understand this sad event in their lives, they are clinging to the truth that God knows more and better than they do. I spent the rest of the evening pondering this loss of another grandchild so very soon after Dedra's loss. I did not spend my time on those empty questions of "Why?" Sometimes there are no answers to why. Maybe, God will have a question-and-answer time in heaven, but I doubt it. I think that when we get to heaven, we will be so enamored by the appearance of the Lord Jesus Christ that the questions of this present life will not matter. I am more interested in the "what" questions that circulate around this unpleasant experience. What is God up to in our family as we grieve over two grandchildren who have been taken from us in such a short period of time? What is God teaching me in these events? What part of these deaths will God use to honor His name and work in His kingdom? It is too soon to speculate on the answers to these questions. I may never know the answers, and I am content not to know. You see, God has done a wonderful work in my heart since my first experience with loss and grief. But I don't waste my life asking the "Why" questions. I do not live by answers. I live by His faithful promises. I do not have many solutions; I just trust Him with His plan in my life as well as in the lives of the members of my family.

It is not by coincidence that earlier in the week I read again about my friend Job. He lost his entire family in one day. He set for me a great truth regarding losing precious people and possessions in life. It is said of Job that in all of his losses he did not sin by blaming God (1:22). Job said, "The Lord gave and the Lord has taken away; blessed be the name of the Lord" (1:21).

My mind raced to the story of David after he experienced the death of a little boy he had with Bathsheba. David's response is brilliant and serves as a teaching tool for anyone who experiences the loss of a child. The response of David is in 2 Samuel 12:23: "But now he is dead; why should I fast? Can I bring him back again? I shall go to him, but he shall not return to me."

As I lay my head upon the pillow that night, I expressed the same hope as Job and David. I thought of how God is still in control of my little family. I expressed my trust in His good plan for us. I thanked God for all my grandchildren — four on earth and two in heaven. I thought of how I cannot allow grief to set in and control my mind. I must move on with joyful expectation that I will be in heaven with that grandchild one day. I thought of how blessed I am, not because of what I have in possessions, but I am blessed because of the One who has my name written in the palm of His hand. So, this Christmas, I will hang two stockings on the mantel. One will be made of both blue and pink material, and on that stocking the name simply states "Baby Sain." The other stocking will be the color of blue, and the name on that one is "Baby Wheeler."

This time last year I had four grandchildren. This year of 2017, God has blessed me with two more grandchildren for a total of six. I now have six — four of whom I can love, feel, see, and spoil rotten — two of whom God has in His possession, and I know they are extremely cared for and well loved. Yes, I agree with Job, the Lord gives and the Lord takes away. Blessed be the name of the Lord.

I am writing a few days after being with my grieving daughter and son-in-law. They have felt the harsh blow of the reality of knowing they will never have the privilege of seeing their stillborn son grow up. My mind raced to Chapter 3, verses 32-33 in the Lamentations. I must review it for my own edification in light of what my heart experienced in trying to minister to my daughter and son-in-law.

Verse 32 says, "Though He brings grief, He also shows compassion because of the greatness of His unfailing love" (NLT). This verse allows we who grieve an insight into the character of a holy, just, and merciful God. These verses when taken together offer the hurting heart a new hope because of God's nature. Grief isn't His final word; compassion is.

Verses 31-33 tell us that (1) our grief is only a period in our time span. Grieving is not a life sentence. Just as with a container of milk, our grief has an expiration date. This is good news and hope to those who question if this sadness will ever come to an end.

Verse 32 speaks of how God's great compassion is greater than our pain of grief. He is compassionate because of His love that is directed toward us. This answers the questions of "Will I be able to survive this darkness? And does God love me in my sorrow?" Verse 33 supports the nature of God's love, for He does not take joy in sending afflictions. We can face our grief with joy as we know of God's love and compassion and that there is a limitation to the sorrow.

Grieving hearts must understand that God affords us hope during this time. His affection is available to us. His comfort is provided in these words. His character is clothed in such love that He never releases pain just for the sake of seeing people hurt. I found great strength in these verses as I watched my family suffer grief. I know we are secure in His compassionate love. This is a beautiful message to share!

Verse 32 grabs my attention because it displays two characteristics of God's nature. He brings grief. He shows compassion. There is a dichotomy within this insightful verse that draws our attention to an often unfamiliar observance of His character. John Piper says, "God is completely consistent in all He does, but He is also very complicated. You will never find a contradiction in His character, but you will often have to work hard to see how different aspects of who He is relate to one another."[8]

Christians take very little issue with the loving and tender compassionate nature of God. I am very content with the truth of a compassionate God, both due to the truth of Scripture and to personal experience. It is often hard to accept the other seemingly contradictory description of God bringing grief. One often wonders how can God bring grief and then show loving compassion sometime during the grief period? A bolder question might be, "Is God responsible for grief? Is He the one who causes grief regardless of the type of loss — whether it be from the hand of another person or the tragic loss of something we hold dear? Personally, I had never seen God in the light of Him causing grief until my study of Lamentations. How grateful I am that God continues to show us another side of His being! I do not claim to have all the answers about this description of God's character. However, I have come to some personal resolutions that have helped me. I want to mention a few in hopes that you who have loved and now grieve over a loss will be encouraged.

God is sovereign. I define sovereign: God is and acts as king over this kingdom (i.e., universe). He has supreme authority over all past, present, and future activities. There is no room for debate. He rules and overrules. He has no equal to His rule or authority. He has control over all things. He is all-powerful, and all-present. He has full knowledge of the past, present and future events of this universe. Upon the heels of this truth is the fact that because He is in total control, it must be recognized that He permits, or at least allows, grief to enter into the human experience. If God did not allow or permit the grief, it would mean that God has lost His title of sovereign God, thus relegating Him to being weak or finite. Such an idea is unthinkable among sound biblical teaching. Nothing happens outside God's will.

Honestly, I have recoiled in the past as I have heard people blame God for the death of a loved one or the destruction due to a natural disaster. I felt so inadequate as I attempted to rescue God's reputation from being blamed because of grief. Well, God is large enough to defend Himself, and He does so in His word. Here are a few of the passages that support His sovereign rule:

Psalm 115:3	Romans 8:28
Proverbs 16:9	2 Chronicles 20:6
Psalm 75:6-7	Isaiah 46:10
Romans 11:36	Psalm 135:6-10
Ephesians 1:11	Psalm 22:28

Because God is sovereign, He has all authority to permit grief to enter into our lives. Creatures of God (i.e., humans) have no right to reject God's allowance of grief if we view ourselves as His servants. Servants have no right to reject the King's authority for we acknowledge our position of submission to Him. God has all authority to bring grief into our experience. This can be harsh to the grieving person. To say to those who grieve a loss, "Well, God allowed this, get over it," is unsympathetic and shows no likeness of Christ. It portrays God as a monster and one who enjoys the suffering of people (Lamentations 3:33). That truth must be treated with another truth about God's character. The positive side is that God shows great compassion as well because of His great love for people. Therefore, all that God does allow or permit is to be seen through His nature of love for people. (Lamentations 3:32b) Out of love, God will act right and just toward those who suffer grief and whatever God allows them to lose that causes this grief. We can rest with assurance that He has a purpose and plan that will be good for us and bring glory for Him (Romans 8:28). God's final action in our lives is not grief but loving compassion.

There is a beautiful word picture that shows us God's sovereign power to achieve His plan for us. Hebrews 1:3 states, "And upholding all things by the word of His power." The word "uphold" means to carry or bear. The picture is that of a ship being carried along by the wind and waves of the sea. The beauty of this phrase is that God is seen as being involved in His world. He is actively carrying this world to a future goal and plan. We are part of His plan. He is aware and involved in our lives.

Ephesians 1:11 reinforces this thought. God is in control. He permits grief into our lives. He loves us in spite of what we think, and He has a wonderful purpose for our inward pain. This verse states, "He makes everything work out according to His plan" (NLT). This verse deepens the thought of Hebrews 1:3, because God not only carries the universe along to its complete destination, but He also brings about things in accordance with His purpose. Page 42 of John Piper and Justin Taylor's book *Suffering and Sovereignty of God* reminds us God is at work bringing all things to His desired plan.[9] Here is where Romans 8:28 becomes most personal to us. God turns those negatives in life into positives for us because God's purpose for us is good. God gets glory for those events because His people honor Him as they respond to Him in faith. We may never know the full purposes of God carrying us through grief. He never asks us for permission to do so. Nor, does He show us the set of blueprints He has for our lives. He does not have to, for He is God. Although we might not see or understand His plan, we can rest assured that we can trust His plan for us as well as His love for us. A much wiser person once said, "When you cannot trace the hand of God, you can always trust His heart."

The story of Joseph is found in Genesis, Chapters 37-50. We are given a very insightful look as to how God turns the evil intentions of people into something very beneficial for Joseph as well as for the Hebrew nation (Genesis 45:5, 7-8). Genesis 50:19-20 is the high-water mark in the story of God's power to turn hurtful experiences into wonderful blessings.

If anyone had a right to be bitter toward life, it was Joseph. His jealous brothers hated and plotted to kill him. They reconsidered and instead decided to sell him into slavery. Joseph was separated from his loving father and taken to Egypt. He was purchased by Potiphar, an

Egyptian officer, to serve in his house. Soon his master's wife falsely accused him of attempted rape. Although he was innocent, his angry master put Joseph into prison where he was virtually forgotten about.

With all the mistreatment from his family and others, Joseph never complains. He never releases a hateful remark toward anyone. Without question Joseph stands as a sterling example to everyone who struggles with life's inequities.

Joseph was not perfect. He was thoroughly human. I'm sure he had moments of confusion as to why God would allow these ill treatments to come his way in life. Perhaps Satan whispered to him that he had every right to be angry at those who mistreated him. However, there was no time where Joseph responded to his plight in any way other than confidence in God. His response to all the injustices directed toward him begs the question, "How did Joseph face these issues without getting stuck in the bitterness of it all?"

We are fortunate to have the Scripture, which gives us some insightful information that will help us overcome the feeling of great loss and move forward in life with a positive attitude. The context of Genesis 50:19-21 is that Joseph and his brothers, along with his father, Jacob, have been reunited and reconciled as a family in the land of Egypt. As time passes Jacob dies. Joseph's bothers believed that Joseph would surely seek revenge on them now that Jacob was dead. They assume that Joseph will release his pent-up anger upon them. The reaction of Joseph is completely different from what they expected. Again, what did Joseph do to truly move beyond his hurt to be helpful to his brothers?

First, Joseph trusted God to "settle the score" with his brothers (verse 19). Joseph asked the question, "Am I in the place of God?" The answer to the question is a resounding "NO!" Joseph determined that he would not take God's place as the judge over his brothers. Joseph had a deep confidence in God's full knowledge of the intentions of their hearts. Joseph entrusted God to "settle the score" and to vindicate him. This allowed Joseph to forgive and be free from the desire to get even through revenge. Joseph's action of forgiveness toward his brothers gave him freedom to live with the knowledge that vengeance belonged to God and not to him.

Second, Joseph was able to release the past so he could relish the present (verse 19c). Joseph told his brothers, "Fear not." Long before his brothers came to him for help, Joseph had forgiven his family. He let the past remain in the past. Joseph's ability to release the past through forgiveness was evident when he encouraged his brothers not to be afraid of him. He intended no harm to them. By way of contrast, his brothers were never free from the past. They thought that the absence of Jacob would be Joseph's opportunity to lash out at them. There will not be freedom as long as there is fear. Those who release the past also cast out the fear. Those who forgive others are able to build bridges to people instead of walls.

One thing that is worthy to note is that Joseph did not have to let go of the past. He chose to. Joseph did not need his brothers. At this period in Joseph's life, he was a powerful and prominent person. He could have taken the road that many do when insulted by people. He could have chosen the natural human response of staying in the past and holding on to the bitterness as a baby clings to a toy. Joseph did not choose to act naturally, but supernaturally. He did not choose to act as simply human, for he desired to act as God would. He forgave the past and moved on in life. We have the same choice before us in times of loss.

Releasing the past while relishing the future can be likened to reading a book. If we become stuck in one chapter because we enjoy that particular chapter, we will never turn the page to begin the next chapter of the book. So it is with life. If we are stuck in the past because it makes us feel powerful to hold a grudge or it makes us the victim of circumstances, and we will never advance in life. We must turn the page of that chapter and move forward into the future.

Third and last, Joseph was able to move beyond the pain of mistreatment to see the plan of God (verse 20). The plan was for Joseph to be in the position to save many people from death because of famine. From a youth, Joseph knew God had a plan for his life. Joseph knew he could trust God to develop the plan throughout every situation of his life. He understood that life's detours and roadblocks did not mean that God had forsaken him or forfeited the plan God had designed for his life. Joseph's calm assurance in God's plan for his life allowed him the confidence to say to his brothers, "[Y]e thought evil against me, but God meant it unto good" (KJV).

God in His wisdom will permit the hard times to come into our lives. Grief is certainly a hard place in life. However, the story of Joseph serves as an example that when we look beyond the pain, we will see God working out His plan in our lives. God is holding us by His grace. He is teaching and developing us by His wisdom. In His time, He will allow us to pass through the grief more refined and positioned to complete His plan for our lives.

The Book of Esther is another validation of God's control over experiences in the lives of His people. Although the book has no mention of God, you can see His handiwork upon every page. God's sovereignty is highlighted as He removes a reigning queen from the kingdom of Ahasuerus and arranges an unknown, yet beautiful girl named Esther to be the queen of King Ahasuerus. In the providence of God, He allowed the uncle of Esther to accompany her to the kingdom. That uncle, Mordecai, became the guardian of Esther after her parents' death. Both he and Esther were Jews who were being assimilated into a Gentile kingdom; it is the favor of God upon these two "strangers" that impresses us.

Mordecai found comfort sitting outside the king's palace while staying abreast of the affairs of Esther. Mordecai overheard two men who were angry at the king and plotted an assassination of Him. Mordecai told the plan to Esther who in turn made the king privy to it. Both men were given the sentence of death for their atrocious scheme. Mordecai was given credit for saving the king's life. Did these events unfold by "luck," consequence, or happenstance? No. God was carrying out His desired plan all the time.

A shadier character enters the story whose name is Haman. He is a powerful figure who has the respect of the people as well as the authority from the king. Haman demanded that the servants in the palace bow and show respect for him. Everyone followed protocol except Mordecai. Mordecai, being a Jew, would give allegiance to no person but God. His convictions place him into a confrontation with Haman. Prideful Haman took his hatred out not only upon Mordecai, but upon all the Jews. His desire was to kill all the Jews in the land.

Haman went before the king and encouraged him to make a law that on a certain date all Jews would be destroyed. The wish of Haman became law throughout the land. From our viewpoint it appears that God has lost control and been overthrown by a hateful man and an unsuspecting king. We wonder, Where is God's power to save these innocent people from death? However, this is not the end of God's story. Mordecai is highly troubled upon hearing of the law that sets in motion the death of all Jews. When Mordecai was asked why he was so upset, he told one of Esther's servants about the plot to destroy the Jews. Hatach, Esther's servant relayed the message to her, which stated that she must go into the king and plead for her people. This was very difficult for Esther. The rule was that anyone who entered into the presence of the king without permission would possibly be greeted with the death penalty. This included the queen. Mordecai told her the raw truth of the matter as he explained that she would not escape this death simply because she was the queen. She must not hold her voice. Mordecai informed her that God will save the Jews, but her family will suffer a sad end.

Only because of the grace of God, Esther was granted an audience with the king. Upon her acceptance into the king's court, she made a request that Haman be invited to a social gathering that she was planning. This request was granted. Haman swelled with pride as he thought how great he was to be at the top of the guest list and invited to the queen's banquet. His pride and hatred for Mordecai made him a fool as he listened to the advice of his wife and friends. They suggested that gallows be made for the purpose of hanging Mordecai because of his refusal to bow to Haman.

In Esther 6, the working of God begins to show more clearly. That night the king could not sleep. In order to chase away his insomnia, he called for the records of history to be read to him. By the guidance of God, the section chosen to be read to the king was about how a man named Mordecai told of a plot to kill the king and thus saved the king's life. King Ahasuerus discovered that Mordecai had never been rewarded for his bravery and loyalty. The one person out of all people given the task of broadcasting and showing honor to Mordecai was none other than his enemy, Haman. Haman was humiliated that he had to show favor to the man he hated so vigorously. When he arrived at home and told of his day at the office, his wife and advisors told him that since Mordecai is a Jew, he could not overcome him but would be defeated by him.

In deep despair, Haman still looked forward to the banquet that he felt privileged to attend. At the party, Esther began to speak to the king. She revealed her Jewish ancestry and told of the plan by Haman to destroy her people. The king was wroth and momentarily walked outside. Haman pleaded for mercy to Esther. He followed her to her room and fell on her bed. With perfect timing the king walked in and saw him on Esther's bed and accused him of trying to seduce the queen. That night Haman was hung from the very gallows that he intended to be used for the hanging of Mordecai. The king gave Haman's property to Esther and gave Mordecai a high position in the kingdom. He superseded the law to destroy the Jews so that their lives were saved and great rejoicing occurred throughout the country.

This story reveals the involvement, control and influence upon the events and lives of the people in the Book of Esther. God's hand is like that of a weaver who incorporates the fibers of life's events into a beautiful tapestry for people to see His perfect design. This story has application for those who grieve. There are moments that seem hopeless and absent of God's involvement. These are times of uncertainty, fear, and emotional darkness. Take encouragement from Esther's life and realize that God is at work behind the scenes. He is moving events and people in ways that will be a wonderful honor to Him and a blessing for you.

Lamentations 3:32 states the following: "Though He brings grief, He also shows compassion because of the greatness of His unfailing love" (NLT).

The nature of our loving God is one of balance. He allows grief into our lives for purposes often known only to Him. We should respond to His sending grief into our lives with a confident trust that He is in full control of the events of our lives, and His ways and wisdom are higher than ours. He has us on a purposeful plan that He will see to its end. God knows how tender we are in periods of grief, so He tempers the time of grief with compassion because He loves us beyond our greatest dreams.

There are many ways that God shows us compassion as we go through the pain of grief. He is immensely able to show compassion to us in many ways. God often consoles us through His written word. There are several Bible stories of how He came to those great and small in their time of need and gave them hope and encouragement. Both past and present writers have been used of God to give insight into the ways of healing from grief in helpful books. God often has renewed old friendships through social media to connect those who have experienced great loss in their lives and through that renewed friendship they become instruments of healing. God puts people into our lives to be an extension of Christ to us. Among other places, these people are found at church, support groups and in the neighborhoods. Last but certainly not least, God has people who are trained counselors who can help us "name" our hurt and understand a way out of the darkness. Pastors are readily available to listen and encourage us and can refer us to people who can help. These people are as lights that God uses to enter our lives and give us a soothing word, an encouraging thought, and the compassion He desires for us. Personally, I have seen the compassion of God displayed in my life many times and through many ways. Each time God shows up through people and experiences, I know it is His reminder to me that He is involved and still deeply loving me with an everlasting love.

God grants us a choice as to how we respond to the grief in our lives. Is that not amazing? Because He is sovereign, He can limit Himself and offer me freedom to respond. Charles Swindoll says:

> The longer I live, the more I realize the impact of attitude on life. Attitude, to me, is more important than facts. It is more important than the past, than education, than money, than circumstances, than failure, than successes, than what other people think or say or do. It is more important than appearance, giftedness or skill. It will make or break a company … a church … a home. The remarkable thing is we have a choice everyday regarding the attitude we will embrace for that day. We cannot

> change our past ... we cannot change the fact that people will act in a certain way. We cannot change the inevitable. The only thing we can do is play on the one string we have, and that is our attitude. I am convinced that life is 10 percent what happens to me and 90 percent of how I react to it. And so it is with you. We are in charge of our attitudes.[10]

God allows us freedom to choose our attitudes toward grief. Therefore, we must focus upon the truth that grief is a temporary experience. It is not a life sentence. Grief can be a doorway to healing for ourselves and helpfulness for others. When we cooperate with God by choosing positive attitudes, God will use the grief to construct us into more effective servants for Him. God will transform our inner pain into an outward expression of His mercy and grace.

The grief requires some action, so use the pain not to panic as if there is no hopeful solution, but as a source of energy that motivates you to act. Sometimes grief entices us to be immobile. Therefore, we do not act in positive ways to deal with grief. To be uninvolved in processing the grief or in working through the process is the path of least resistance, but it leaves one stuck in the pain, which is not emotionally healthy. Also, to choose to become detached emotionally does not lend itself to an opportunity to grow and mature through the grief. Often people try to deny their grief as if it does not exist. They attempt to "check out" of the grief. To act as though one is immune to grief is to be untrue to your feelings. Grief is normal for everyone who has loved and lost someone or something in their life. The truth is that grief will work its way out of your life somehow. It might be denied for a time, but it shows itself in our mental health, our relationship to others and to God. God allows us the opportunity to participate in grief's healing process as we choose to move out of the "stuck" position to become partners with God as we heal.

We must choose positive attitudes about God while we heal. Our understanding of the nature of God, or lack of it, will determine if and how we move toward healing or if we will remain in a place of hopelessness. In short, grief can make us better or bitter. The choice is ours.

My journey with grief began with the loss of four precious relationships in my life. I did not lose all four in one day as Job did, but within a period of one year these treasures of my heart changed forever. I met the first two losses with unwavering faith and confidence that Romans 8:28 would be my "go to" verse for keeping my faith centered in God. Somewhere in the midst of the third and fourth loss, the liar, Satan, began to suggest that God was not fair, that God had abandoned me, and that God did not love me. God might love the world, but He could not love me or else He would not allow these relationships in my life to dissolve. I felt hopeless, angry, and rejected by God. This led me into a state of clinical depression.

I accepted valuable counseling from professionals. I continued to pray and digest Scripture. I gladly took medication to help me function in my life. Yet, I wrestled with the darkness of being hopeless and angry. I dealt with feeling rejected by God and unloved by Him, even as I confidently told others of God's acceptance and love for them.

All my experiences in life for two years were seen through the dirty lens of a faulty perception of God. I perceived God as not accepting me or loving me. The point that I am attempting to make is, it is easy to come to conclusions about God and people that are false but are understood to be true to your experience. The temptation that seduced me in my weakness from my losses and grief was to trust my experiences rather than the truthful promises of God. Yes, I knew better. Yes, I have been a faithful steward of God's word, but for a while I allowed the truth of God's word concerning His character to take second place to my hurtful experiences. I share this story because I do not want anyone to take the path I took. So, in order to help you avoid the potholes that I fell into, do not perceive God's silence and your feeling of being abandoned as His inactivity in your life. A more secure understanding of God's nature is in His promise from Hebrews 13:5 where He says, "I will never leave thee, nor forsake thee" (KJV). And, in John 14:18, Jesus said, "I will not leave you comfortless; I will come to you" (KJV). I do believe that God will permit us to feel forsaken for a while, as He did His son.

However, God may be using the feeling we have to motivate us to seek Him more diligently. The main force for my argument is that in order to overcome these feelings of God's inactivity in our lives, we must focus on the fact of God's promises of His constant presence with us, rather than on our feelings.

In our journey of grief, these unwanted thoughts creep into our minds and seek to erase the security of God's constant love and purpose for us. The truth from God's word is that God has a greater purpose for us than our pain. The promise God gave to Jeremiah is true for all of God's people. "For I know the thoughts that I think toward you, saith the Lord, thoughts of peace and not of evil, to give you an expected end" (Jeremiah 29:11). God has a purpose for us, and He uses grief to mold us into that image of Christ (Ephesians 1:11-12, Romans 8:28-30). Wisdom helps us understand that people are under God's construction at all times. We are, as Jeremiah portrays us, as clay on the potter's wheel being formed by God's good will for us. He shapes us to His particular plan, and His hand is never off of the shaping process (Philippians 1:6).

Besides God's purpose of shaping us into the image of Christ, I can think of two additional ways which show that God has a purpose for our life. Romans 5:2-5 allows us to see how God uses our pain to build Christlike characteristics in us. Paul tells us to trust in the glory or purposes of God during difficult times such as loss/grief. When we are in the crucible of grief, God helps us to lose trust in things and people so that we develop His virtues as we learn to trust in Him. He uses pain and trouble to give us patience or endurance (verse 3).

As God continues to shape us into the likeness of Christ, we must understand that we will change. Grief is a powerful tool to change our attitudes toward others, reaffirm faith in God, ignite a passion to reorder our life's goals and priorities, value friendships, and embrace every precious moment of life. These are good and productive changes. This is the key to moving forward. Put your faith in God's good purposes for you, embrace the changes He sends, and thank Him for His patience and love as He reconstructs you. From my experiences I can tell you that during this inevitable change that comes along with loss, you will learn more about yourself, your faith, and your love for God than if you were on the "golden brick road" of life. God will show you a side of Himself that you could never learn in the comfort of a Bible study group. When He is finished with that phase of your change, you will think, "I never would stand in line for a journey like that again, but I would not take anything for the trip!"

Endurance comes from trials which develop character. Character develops our confident hope in our walk with God. This idea challenges the theology that God is inactive in our lives. The truth is, He is involved and is working His purpose for us.

Another way God uses grief is to help us be in a position of service to others. Second Corinthians 1:3-7 says:

> *Blessed be the God and Father of our Lord Jesus Christ, the Father of mercies and God of all comfort, who comforts us in all our tribulation, that we may be able to comfort those who are in any trouble, with the comfort with which we ourselves are comforted by God. For as the sufferings of Christ abound in us, so our consolation also abounds through Christ. Now if we are afflicted, it is for your*

> *consolation and salvation, which is effective for enduring the same sufferings which we also suffer. Or if we are comforted, it is for your consolation and salvation. And our hope for you is steadfast, because we know that as you are partakers of the sufferings, so also you will partake of the consolation.*

These verses simply give to us a reason for our suffering as well as an encouragement in our personal suffering. God comforts us so that we are able to comfort others. God allows us to feel the pinch of suffering. God wants us to know that He is our greatest source of comfort as He comforts us, and He equips us to give comfort to others.

Our painful experience is profitable when that experience makes us sensitive to the pain of others hurt in life. The God of all comfort acts in grace and mercy to restore us as well as teach us to be aware of other people. God teaches us and sends us into a hurting world often as a wounded and broken minister to be an extension of mercy to others in Jesus' name.

Without an awareness of God's wisdom in selecting pain for us in order to use us, we would often see no good purpose for His giving us a scar in our life. God never wastes pain. He uses our pain to exalt Him as we serve others — even if we remain wounded from our hurt. It is here that Romans 8:28 takes on new meaning for us. Even though at first there is no obvious reason for our plight, God has a plan. He might allow many hurts and losses to break our heart and our selfish will; He can make us a minister to those who grieve. God often works in us while we are in the dark unknown. In His time and fashion, He sheds His light upon the unknown so we can see His purposes.

As we come to understand that God desires to use us to minister to others, we must remember how God has placed people in our lives to minister to us. God's Holy Spirit is our Comforter (John 14:16-18) in our grief. Christ himself is our High Priest who sympathizes with us (Hebrews 4:15). He invites us to cast our cares upon Him for He cares for us (1 Peter 5:7). Isaiah presents Christ as "a man of sorrows and acquainted with grief (53:3). Christ is able to feel with us and for us in our loss as demonstrated when He extended His ministry to Mary and Martha in the loss of Lazarus (John 11:35). Second Corinthians 1:34 heralds God as the God of all comfort. Time does not allow me to present every passage that deals with this truth: When we grieve, the entire Godhead arrives at our hearts to give us the support we need in the times of grief. This shows the richness of God's compassion and care for the hurting hearts of His children. The reality is that if it was not for the Lord, grief would overtake us and consume us. God rescues our hurting hearts. Praise to Him for His mercy.

God is not limited in the many ways He can minister to us. God has a host of ministers that He places in our paths as we travel in grief. People are instrumental in our lives. We need each other, especially in those moments when we feel isolated and think no one cares.

During one of the darkest moments in my life, I asked for and received a six-week sabbatical from my work. The first weekend was spent at The Cove in Asheville, North Carolina, for Bible study and rest. I was completely exhausted to the point that driving was a task. My mind was a battlefield, whereby Satan constantly fed me lies, and my heart was broken at the great losses I had experienced. I was empty.

I wish I could remember her name. Perhaps her name is not as important as what she said and did to minister to me. I remember sitting beside a lady who had brought her mother from Ohio to The Cove for a weekend of spiritual re-fueling. I noticed that she had some reading materials pertaining to the medical field. In our conversation, I said, "You have several medical journals with you. Are you a nurse?" She replied with kindness, "No, I am a children's surgeon in a certain hospital in Ohio. I brought some magazines thinking I might catch up on some reading." I felt like a klutz and quickly apologized if I had offended her for asking her about her job. She was quick to excuse me, and we laughed off my assumption.

Then she said to me words that I will never forget. She said, "You appear to me to be so hurt even to the point that you are empty inside. Back home I take upon myself to care for my pastor, and for this weekend will you allow me to show compassion to you?" I held my tears back for the time and said, "You have a keen sense of discernment, and I would be honored for you to minister to me." From that time this wonderful Christian lady spoke life-giving words from God's word that helped restore my soul. She and her mother made sure they sat with me during mealtimes. She never dug into the circumstances that placed me in darkness. She only encouraged me, prayed for me, and was a source of refreshment for my dry soul.

On the day the conference was over, I thanked her for her allowing God to use her in my life. I told her of how God used her to remind me that He loves me and showed me His loving-kindness through her. I have never met her again. I will see her in heaven one day, and I will tell her again of the wonderful way she encouraged me and allowed God to love me through her.

After returning from The Cove, I began to process the Bible truths that I had gleaned from the conference. I also relished the fact that God positioned me to sit beside a children's surgeon who would be willing to be used of God to speak to me of His love for me. To me, this is overwhelming.

I tell this story to make us aware that God uses people to minister to us. Welcome their ministry into your life. God knows what we need to help our hearts and often it is the voice, the sight and the sound of another person who deeply becomes Jesus to us in life.

In summary, there are several simple facts about God and His love that will help us understand God's involvement in our grief. (1) God may be silent, but He is always active in our life. (2) God is planning a greater purpose for us in our pain. (3) God has placed people in our lives to minister to us.

Lamentations Chapter 3, verses 34-36 form one sentence. These verses of Scripture seek to give clarity to questions that often are not verbalized but are inwardly entertained. God does not enjoy hurting people. He takes no pleasure in allowing painful experience to come upon people (verse 33). He allows the harsh mistreatments and injustices to come upon people, but these actions are not allowed for His pleasure. We live in a cursed world with many afflictions. For Him to step in and prevent every mishap that can come to people would remove human responsibility. Heaven would be less precious if there were no calamities on earth.

In this world, there always will be problems that confront people. Often we make wrong choices and hurt ourselves. At times an enemy will cause us to fall. Although God is aware of everything that happens to us, He does not always prevent these events. This truth is captured in verses 37-39. The writer's point is that God's permissive will is for both good and bad events to come into the life of both saint and sinner in this world. Both good and harsh events come to all people. God allows the rain to fall on the just and the unjust (Matthew 5:45). We should not direct anger toward God when we experience God's punishment for our sin, because evil has placed us in this sad state. Punishment follows our wicked choice, and we should expect no less from a holy God. Therefore, let the complaining stop. Let us praise His love for us and not allow ourselves to become and remain bitter toward God.

In the section of Scripture from verses 40-60, there is a major shift in two ways. The writer changes his style to the first-person plural by using the identifying words "us" and "our." He includes himself in stating the need for people to confess and return to God by repentance. There is another shift that is more important to those who are experiencing times of grief. The tone and character of these verses are considerably different from the previous verses. Jeremiah is hopeful and confident in God's love, faithfulness, and restoration in verses 21-34. He seems to be riding the heights of God's unfailing mercy toward those who grieve. However, verses 40-66 reflect the same tone of hopelessness, darkness, and sorrow as in the first part of Chapter 3. What is wrong? Is Jeremiah bi-polar in his emotions? The answer is, No. He is normal. He is experiencing the same emotional roller coaster that many do as they grieve.

Within the paradigm of grief counseling, there is the vivid display of a cycle of grief. This pattern features breakouts of tears, anxiety, and anger, to moments of joy, hope, and acceptance. This is the time when some question their sanity. These actions are normal and necessary for healing. R. Scott Sullender states there is no consistency in the pain of grief. The waves of pain are alternated by periods of momentary rest. These waves are like those found on a graph. There are highs and lows until these painful moments pass and usher in a calmness of the soul.[11] I think this is exactly what Jeremiah experienced in these verses. Even in this topsy-turvy aspect of the grieving process, God is good. He allows our healing by giving us times of tears. He is gracious and kind to stay the tears and let us have moments of pleasant memories that give us joy. Within that time, we heal and begin to be whole again. This is God at work for us as we grieve.

It is common during this period to experience deeper emotions than tears and joy. These are feelings that cause us to dig deeper into our minds and ask serious questions about ourselves. These are feelings that allow us to grow deeper as a person for they challenge us to come forth with our true inner feeling. Once again, we are not without help in this area.

Elisabeth Kübler-Ross was a psychiatrist who wrote the book entitled *On Death and Dying* in 1969. In that book, she introduced to us the theory of the "five stages of grief." These findings of the stages of grief were based on her research of the feelings of people who were facing terminal illness. These are hypothetical in nature because there is no "one size fits all" in the grief process. Also, since her work, others have listed from two to five stages of grieving. However, these five stages are valuable as we observe the people of Judah in their loss and grief cycle. These five stages are helpful for they allow us the confidence of knowing that as we pass through many of the stages, we are "normal, healthy" human beings that suffer grief, and that others have passed this way before.

It is very important to know that it is possible to go through your grief without experiencing every stage that Kübler-Ross lists. Some people experience only one or two of these stages, and some people might not experience any of them. Also, there is no certain order the grieving person must follow as he or she grieves. The Kübler-Ross model is only a theory, and an individual deserves the right to grieve at their own pace. In fact, Kübler-Ross wrote before her death in 2004, "They [five stages of grief] were never meant to help tuck messy emotions into neat packages. They are responses to loss that many people have, but there is not a typical response to loss, as there is no typical loss. Our grieving is as individual as our lives."[12]

Just as a sidebar, I understand that Elisabeth Kübler-Ross did not profess to be a Christian. In fact, I find material that shows her in opposition to a good and kind God, especially at the end of her life. I also understand that her theory has been criticized by the medical and theological institutions. However, it is still widely accepted as valuable in the study of grief. Remember, the work of Kübler-Ross is a theory, but it can help us understand the grieving process. Dr. Kübler-Ross did have a view of the afterlife, but it would not match a biblical view given in Scripture.

The five stages of grief according to Elisabeth Kübler-Ross are:

Denial: Kübler-Ross states, "Denial is usually a temporary defense and will soon be replaced by partial acceptance."[13]

The first stage of grief is denial. Denial serves as a defense mechanism to protect the individual from too great a shock to his mind. There may be a feeling of numbness. His expression may be one of "this is not happening to me." "This bad report is not mine." In time the person drops his denial and moves to an acceptance of reality.

The second stage of the grief process is anger. Anger: Once the terminally ill patient settles into the truth of his demise, he assumes another stage of grief that Kübler-Ross calls anger. During this stage the patient has feelings of anger, rage, envy, and resentment that are difficult to handle because the anger is misplaced in many directions. Here, people project anger at the doctors, nursing staff, and friends. Everyone seems to share the blame during this stage. In this stage, the patient wants to be heard and recognized as one who is still alive. So, an attempt is made to get attention by behavior. The focus of his anger (e.g., a family member, doctor, etc.) really is not the true problem. The true problem is that he has not yet accepted his eventual death.

The third stage of grieving, according to Kübler-Ross, is bargaining. Kübler-Ross states: "If we have been unable to face the sad facts in the first period and have been angry at people and God in the second phase, maybe we can succeed in entering into some sort of an agreement which may postpone the inevitable happening: 'If God has decided to take us from this earth and He did not respond to my angry pleas, He may be more favorable if I ask nicely.'"[14] Bargaining is really an attempt to postpone the inevitable.

The fourth stage in the grieving process according to Kübler-Ross is depression.[15] During this stage, the terminally ill patient begins to understand that death is certain for him. Often the patient becomes withdrawn from friends. He becomes silent and much of the time is spent in an activity of tears and gloom. People who love the grieving person should share this phase with him. It is a painful process for all to experience, but it allows the patient to disconnect from things he cherishes and find the next stage.

The fifth stage of grief is acceptance. Acceptance at this place in the grieving process the patient has come to a full circle of his grief and has come to terms with the end of his life with a degree of gentle expectation. This should not be mistaken for a happy stage. It is a time of peace and acceptance and is sometimes signaled by the patient's desire to be in a time of quietness or a need to detach oneself from others.[16]

I write of these five stages because they are important to those who grieve as well as to friends who watch a loved one grieve. Sometimes it is good just to hear that we are normal.

In the last paragraph of Chapter 3, verses 53-66, we are given a view of the human side of the prophet. Jeremiah has been treated very harshly by those who oppose him. He finds great comfort in knowing that God sees his suffering. God knows of his enemies' assaults, both physical and verbal. Jeremiah does not believe these attacks upon him are justified. Therefore, he calls out to God for vengeance upon his enemies. In verses 64-66, Jeremiah pleads with God to take revenge upon those who have caused him pain. He goes so far as to ask God to curse them. To put the verse into today's vernacular, Jeremiah asked God to send them to hell. Jeremiah asked for nothing less from God for his enemies than that they be severely punished.

This is not the first time Jeremiah burst forth with a prayer to God to take revenge upon his enemies (Jeremiah 11:20, 12:3, 15:15, 17:18, 19:21-23). The desire to call upon God to repay one's enemy with revenge was common in the Old Testament (Numbers 22:6; Psalm 35:4-8, 40, and 129:5-6). Jeremiah was acting from the position of human feelings of perceived injustices and from the Old Testament understanding of "an eye for an eye" law of retribution.

Jeremiah did not have the advantage of the words of Jesus as He taught us a new way to deal with our enemies (Matthew 5:38-41). Nor did he have the example of how Christ dealt with His oppressors when He was on the cross (Luke 23:33-34). We have fulfillment of Old Testament truth found in the words and lifestyle of Jesus. Therefore, we should understand that Jeremiah acted out of his human spirit and the teachings of the Old Testament. We are called to a higher standard as we deal with our oppressors.

Jeremiah's example teaches us a very important lesson in our journey through grief. He brings to light something that many people experience but seldom admit: inner anger and bitterness. This anger may be directed at their state in life, themselves, others, or even God. It is a very ugly part of us that we like to keep hidden, but the truth is, it often appears in our emotions and relationships. We must admit that forgiveness plays a great part in the healing of our grief. Unforgiveness is like a cancer in our souls that little by little eats away our spiritual, emotional, and even physical wellbeing. If left unchecked, we become spiritual and emotional invalids. Unforgiveness must be dealt with or there will be no future progress in healing from grief. There is great freedom as we forgive those whom we believe have hurt us in life. This freedom is not for our enemies. Rather it is for those of us who hold anger and resentment. To release someone from an offense is the greatest liberty anyone can experience. The word "forgive" is defined by Websters II New College Dictionary as to excuse for a fault or offense: 1. Pardon. 2. To renounce anger or resentment against. 3. To absolve from payment of (i.e., a debt).

Personally, I think number 3 is a solid biblical definition for the word "forgive." We think there is power in holding a debt against someone who has wounded us. We think we have leverage or control over them because they owe us a debt of apology. How foolish we are to think that because many times our offender never thinks he has offended us, much less that he owes us an apology. All along we carry the baggage of resentment when we think someone owes us for an offense made toward us.

There is tremendous freedom when we simply forgive and cancel any debt someone owes us. Write across the debt "cancelled" or "paid in full." Release him from whatever it might be we think he is indebted to us for. That's freedom. This is possible because of what our Lord has done for us. All of our debt of sin toward Him was cancelled because of Christ's work on the cross. That, in fact, is what made forgiveness available to us. God does not hold us in debt because Christ has paid for our sins against Him. When you and I seek to hold someone in debt to us by not forgiving him for some offense, we simply try to do something to him that God Himself does not do.

Unforgiveness is like an uncontrollable relative that we try to hide from more well-to-do friends. We know the relative is in our house, but we dare not introduce him to other people for fear of shame or embarrassment. We do all we can to keep him quiet and out of sight. Regardless of our effort to conceal our relative, he reveals himself and often brings with him problems such as depression, anger, bitterness, and other sorts of physical ailments.

What can one do to combat this feeling of unforgiveness that often harms self rather than the person unforgiveness is harbored toward? I will briefly mention a few ideas that can help us forgive someone from a past trespass and allow us to move forward. The truth is that our forgiveness must come from our heart. We must make a volitional and truthful choice to spiritually and emotionally release a person from his debt to us. We let the offense go as well as we let the offender. We let him off the hook. We take our hands off of the debt line. We no longer keep score for we entrust the score card to the Lord who forgave us. These are the key elements in forgiveness.

Here are some ways that can help us begin the work of forgiveness toward someone. Consider a situation where the person whom you have not forgiven is deceased. You might find it helpful to go to his grave (I know this is morbid) and tell him that you no longer hold him in debt to you for his offense. Hold nothing back as you release your pain. Tell him that you seek to move forward to bring closure to your grief, and you believe forgiving him will help you get to that place. Forgive him from your heart! Turn him loose and walk away in a newfound freedom.

The second idea is also applicable to those who are deceased. Sit down and write a letter. Express to that person why you have held a spirit of unforgiveness toward him. Tell him every dirty detail of the hows and whys he hurt you. Hold nothing back in your letter. This writing must be a full catharsis of the soul. After you have fully expressed yourself, pray over it. Ask God to forgive you for feelings of unforgiveness and then find that inward freedom as you release that person from debt. As you complete the letter, you might choose to destroy it as a symbolic gesture of your total forgiveness to that person.

Norman Wright, in his book entitled *Recovering from the Losses of Life,* suggests that two chairs are set up facing each other. One chair is occupied by you, and then you imagine the other chair is occupied by the person who has offended you.[17] Read your list of offenses to that imagined person with force and voice inflection that shows the depth of your hurt and concern. Take your time. Be sure to verbalize every part of the pain. At the end of the session, turn to God. Ask God to help you heal from the offense. Thank Him for allowing you to be honest as you spoke. Then thank God for His knowledge of your hurt and His grace to move forward in life to a more peaceful mindset.

These ideas are only a few of many that can help them forgive those who have hurt them. There are other methods. Whatever one finds to help move from being stuck in unforgiveness should be pursued. Please keep focused upon truth that must never be compromised as you think about forgiving others. No one has a right or reason to hold unforgiveness over anyone when God, through Jesus Christ, has forgiven everyone who has asked to be forgiven. When we refuse to forgive others, we assume a position that God Himself does not assume. We never have a right to play God and withhold forgiveness just because it makes us feel powerful over someone. You and I can find ultimate freedom when we have been forgiven and are generous to forgive others. Forgiveness is one key to happiness.

I sense that Jeremiah had a "come to Jesus" meeting in verses 4-49. It was a radical moment when he began to see the plight of his people as he rightly should. Perhaps this revelation of God began in Chapter 3, verses 22-26 and again in Chapter 3, verses 31-33. Seeing God aright afforded him the clarity of understanding toward himself and his people. These truths have a teaching moment for us as we examine them in the light of the grieving experience.

What is evident in verses 40-59 is that Jeremiah finds the strength to gaze deeply into the reason as to why the people have continued to be punished by God. This is so very important for it is vital to the healing process of grief. Jeremiah becomes active in the healing of himself and the people as he becomes more introspective in his writing. This point must not be overlooked for he becomes personally involved. It happens often in the final stage of the grief cycle of acceptance. Some time had passed from the trauma of losing many precious things. Perhaps his emotions were beginning to settle. His mind was clearer, so he began to see the goodness of God and the real reason for the continued punishment. No longer could God be blamed for being unkind or uninvolved. Now Jeremiah faces the truth: The people are being punished continually because they have never repented. Therefore, God has not forgiven them because they have not asked. He does not listen to their prayers. Jeremiah calls upon the people to recognize their guilt, lack of repentance and responsibility to repent before God. The sin of the people resulted in God's judgment. As a result of their prideful rebellion, God had rejected them as garbage and refused to hear their prayers for help. To add insult, the nations around them showed their disdain for Judah. God's judgment came because of the people's sin and not because God was unkind or unloving to them. Tears filled Jeremiah's eyes as he thought on this.

The point that I stress is that in the grief, you and I must become an active part in mending our souls. This truth empowers us to reject the idea that we are the victim, or that we are powerless to help ourselves from the grip of grief. In order to help in our healing, we have to take command of our thoughts, emotions and feelings, and we have to stop seeing ourselves as victims. In other words, we hold the key to our recovery. We can get help from many sources, and we should. But in the end, we will have to do the "heavy lifting." It is called personal involvement, and it will be the hardest work anyone will ever do. Jeremiah made the decision to take charge of his thoughts, and as he did one can see how much difference it made.

Here are some simple things that you can do to help yourself:

- *Join a grief recovery class.* Perhaps your local church offers this opportunity. Ask a local funeral home if it offers help groups. Sometimes these groups are found through hospice and palliative care centers. Also, it is possible that community centers offer this service for those who grieve. These places offer helpful insights to recover from grief but also keep you in touch with a people group that you can relate to.

- *Find a godly counselor.* Your pastor may be trained to help, but if he isn't comfortable or if you are not comfortable, ask him to refer you to a Bible-based, Christ-centered counselor. A quick search online under Focus on the Family will afford you their numbers. They will recommend a counselor in your area you can call for an appointment.
- *Read books on grief.* I recommend Christian authors first and do so because they give Christian principles to help to focus on our great physician — Jesus, who is our ultimate Healer. However, I do not rule out secular writers that are helpful as well. Go to the local library and browse through the grief section. The internet sources such as Amazon offer both secular and Christian authors on the subject of grief.
- *Begin to journal.* This was a very difficult decision for me. However, after writing out my feelings, hurts, goals, and dreams I found it to be helpful. No one, including my wife, is allowed to look at these personal reflections. Some of my writings are far too private and honest for anyone to see. I have ordered they be destroyed at my death. There is a release in the inner soul as we write out our thoughts.
- *Reconnect with God.* During the grief period, it is very easy to focus inwardly upon life's injustices and how God is not fair to us. During this time, we might be prone to place our discipline of faith in God on the "to do list," but continue to let it lie dormant in our hearts. We must remind ourselves that it is we who have disconnected from His company, and we must return as Jeremiah urged his countrymen to do.

> The reasons for this need to reconnect to God are legion. I will give only two. One reason is simply that God has designed us for the capacity to fellowship with Him. When we decide that our relationship with Him is not necessary for whatever reason, we break with our greatest provision in healing. The next step is to become more confused, agitated, and more rebellious toward our Great Physician. Delores Kuenning writes: "Our reasoning also tells us that when we violate the God-given commandments — which really are positive statements designed to help us live a healthy, uncomplicated lives — we create the conditions that can wreak havoc with our personal lives."[18]

The God who so meticulously designed us knows very well that we must find healing from grief in His companionship.

A second reason we must reconnect with God is that He gives us a true picture of His character. Without a doubt, there is an element of anger during the grieving period. When our anger is directed at God, our initial response might be to avoid fellowship with Him. This is a critical junction in the road toward healing for it is here that you will decide to react to the grief by going AWOL on Christ, or you will choose to stay with Christ and learn His character.

The Apostle Paul said in Philippians 3:10-11, "That I may know Him, and the power of His resurrection, and the fellowship of His sufferings, being made conformable unto His death; If by any means I might attain unto the resurrection of the dead" (KJV). His great desire was to know Christ and the power of His resurrection and fellowship of His suffering. To know Him is to become like Him. Lamentations Chapter 3 is full of truth concerning the beautiful character of God.

Allow me the pleasure of giving you a general synopsis of some of the truths of God's wonderful character from Lamentations Chapter 3.

Verses 1-20: There are sometimes that God will permit a sense of lostness, darkness, loneliness, and hopelessness to fill your minds. This is a horrible time for the believer whose experience does not equal out to his theology of a loving, ever-present God. This darkness is real and often challenges the most faithful believer. However, no one should be surprised at this intentional darkness that pervades the soul. The psalmist wrote of it often. Psalms 13, 22, 44, and 88 are a few of the reminders of people who know of the dark times of life. Our Lord spoke of His forsakenness from the cross (Mark 15:34). Isaiah 54:7-8 says God often will step back for a period of time to get our attention so you and I might search for Him with a pure heart and Christ-centered focus. In those moments of feeling hopeless and alone, God gains our full attention. He speaks, and we are quick to listen. Jeremiah references the forsakenness in Lamentations 3:44.

Verses 21-27 feature messages of hope, love, and the mercies of the faithfulness of God. The grieving soul finds great strength in the goodness of God's mercies that are present on a daily basis. God is good as we wait expectantly upon Him and submit our lives to Him in the painful and dark grief process. Each morning we are met with His vast supply of blessings that are our daily bread to help us overcome the present challenges.

Verses 31-39 tell us more of the character of God. He does not leave us forever. He brings grief and compassion because of His consistent love. Our journey with God in life as well as in grief is a series of blessings and buffetings. The journey is never stagnant. The journey to wellness is filled with ups and downs, but the progress must always be forward. I am reminded of Job 2:10 as he replies to his bitter wife as she challenged him to "Curse God and die." Job's reply is profound as he says, "Should we accept only good things from the hand of God and never anything bad?" (NLT). Jeremiah spoke truth as he said that God brings grief as well as compassion. He never enjoys hurting people. In the grieving heart there is hurt, but our Lord does not enjoy inflicting pain. He does, however, use the pain to move us to Himself.

Jeremiah gives insight into the permissive will of God in verse 37. He allows both good and bad to enter our lives. He will not alter nature to keep us from harm. There are consequences to our choices, and He allows those events to happen. The wonderful truth is that when God allows the pain for whatever reason, He will never waste it. He uses the pain to produce His quality of character in us.

There is another bit of truth concerning the character of God in verses 40-63. God allows us to become involved in helping ourselves. We can cry out, and He will hear, but the truth is we make the deliberate choice to move through our grief. We are not left alone in the healing of our soul, for God is our healer. We must remember that God will use us as we change our course of thought to bring healing. Both God and we are responsible for our healing through grief.

I wanted to revisit these characteristics of God from Lamentations 3 for this purpose. Your theology concerning the nature of God will have a great effect upon your grief recovery. When you see your grief from God's characteristics of grace, love, mercy, and compassion, you know that He is involved in the process of maturing you into the knowledge and likeness of Himself. He allows us to know Him in suffering death to ego and pride, and as well to know His life-giving resurrection. Many of us never grow in times of blessing. We grow in the "beat downs" of life. In those seasons of grief, God is at work, loving us into His likeness.

As you honor Him in submitting to His purpose for your grief, you pay allegiance to Him. You exhibit trust and confidence that He is an all-wise, all-knowing, ever-present God who can be trusted. You set forth an example to others of the indwelling Christ affording you His strength to move forward through the grief process.

Notes

1. F.B. Huey Jr., *The New American Commentary* (Nashville: Broadman Press, 1993), 471.

2. Larry Copeland, USA Today, October 8, 2014.

3. James C. Dobson, *When God Doesn't Make Sense* (Wheaton: Tyndale House Publishers Inc., 1993), 26.

4. Granger E. Westberg, *Good Grief* (Minneapolis: Fortress Press, 1997), 29.

5. "6 Common Depression Types," Harvard Health Publications, January 2017, https://www.health.harvard.edu/mind-and-mood/six-common-depression-types.

6. Huey Jr., *The New American Commentary,* 474.

7. Huey Jr., Ibid.

8. John Piper, "He Will Not Cast Off Forever," September 23, 2014, https://www.desiringgod.org/labs/he-will-not-cast-off-forever.

9. John Piper and Justin Taylor, *Suffering and the Sovereignty of God,* (Wheaton: Crossway, 2006), 42.

10. Charles Swindoll, message at Dallas Theological Seminary, October 18, 2016, https://www.youtube.com/watch?v=fPVKsrg8POI.

11. R. Scott Sullender, *Grief and Growth* (New York: Paulist Press, 1985), 56.

12. Melinda Smith, Lawrence Robinson, and Jeanne Segal, "Coping with Grief and Loss," https://www.helpguide.org/articles/grief/coping-with-grief-and-loss.htm.

13. Elisabeth Kübler-Ross, *On Death and Dying* (New York: Macmillan Publishing Co., 1969), 35-36.

14. Ibid., 72.

15. Ibid., 73.

16. Ibid, 102.

17. Norman Wright, *Recovering from the Losses of Life* (Toronto:

Spire Publishing, 2000), 172.

18. Delores Kuenning, *Helping People Through Grief* (Minneapolis: Bethany House Publishers, 1987), 20.

Chapter 4
PLAUSIBILITY

Reading Chapter 4 of Lamentations reminds me of traveling through a mountainous region. There is the struggle to push your way to the high peak, catch a view of the beauty of all that is beyond, and then there is the experience of the downward journey. Chapter 3 is the apex of Lamentations, especially verses 22-24. Chapters 4 and 5 are the downward trip from the mountain peak. Jeremiah's voice is calmer. His heart is settled because he has discovered that wonderful hope that only a faithful, loving, and merciful God can give in the grief process.

Chapter 4 is also written in an alphabetic acrostic. The first line of every two-lined stanza starts with the next letter of the Hebrew alphabet. The difference between Chapter 4 and the previous chapters is that Chapter 4 has two-line stanzas, whereas Chapters 1, 2 and 3 have three-line stanzas. This signals that the writer is coming to a conclusion of the subject.

Chapter 4 and Chapter 2 are very similar in describing the horrible situation. Many of the pictures Jeremiah paints for us in Chapter 4 are reminders of the terrible conditions of which the Jews suffered. It is easy to understand that these writings come from someone who has had a front-row seat to the judgment of God upon the nation (4:1).

Jeremiah begins with the word "how" as he did in Chapter 1,

verse 1 and Chapter 2, verse 1. The story line of suffering and pain is repeated, but this chapter is different in that he gives us the reason for the suffering. It is the work of a wise counselor that helps us name the pain that is released in our heart due to grief. Just putting a name on the pain helps us to understand our situation better and moves us out of the "stuck position" and on to healing.

The purpose of Chapter 4 is to identify the reason for the suffering judgment of God upon the people of Zion. The suffering of the people was great, and the reason for the suffering was because of the sinful rebellion of the false prophets, priests, and godless civil leaders (4:13, 2:9). Jeremiah writes with a piercing tone and calls out the reason the nation experienced such punishment.

There is a natural outline in Chapter 4. The outline is as follows:

- The Description of Their Pain (verses 1-11)
- The Defilement of the Priests and Prophets (verses 12-16)
- The Despair of the People (verses 17-20)
- The Declaration of the Future Punishment (verses 21-22)

The description of the pain of the people is revealed to us in the first eleven verses of Chapter 4. He begins in verse 1 as he did in Chapter 1, verse 1 and Chapter 2, verse 1. The present condition of the city is in shambles. Two possessions of the temple have been changed. The "most fine gold" is now dimmed, and the glitter is gone from it. The stones of the sanctuary are poured out on every street. One can only imagine the once glowing array of gold and precious jewels that at one time decorated the temple are now tarnished by the dust of the streets of Jerusalem.

Another possession of the temple is the people (verse 2). The people are described as precious and equal in their weight to gold. Now their present state is that of a common clay pot whose appearance is dull and normal. There is a distinct difference between the descriptions of the people who were once called valuable but are now compared to a throwaway pot of no value.

Jeremiah continues his description of the depravity of the people with the example of the mothers who lost their natural instinct to care for their children and became as base as their animal counterparts. Mothers neglected their young as would an ostrich. The famine had reached the point of no food or water, and children were dying as the result. If bread were available, no one would be generous enough to offer it even to a starving child. The graphic seen in verse 10 is that of gaunt starvation to the point where people turned to cannibalism for survival.

Jeremiah remembers days of abundance when people had food in great supply. They dressed in purple as did the people of richness and royalty. Now those days of plenty are turned to poverty. Those who ate the fine foods are scavenging for mere morsels they can find. Those people who once dressed in garments of purple now "dumpster dive" for food and clothing. Jeremiah compares the suffering of Jerusalem to that of Sodom. He says the condition of Jerusalem is even greater because of the longevity of the suffering. Sodom's suffering came and went, but not so with Jerusalem because it lingered.

The ravishing famine is no respecter of people for now verse 7 speaks of the youth. Noble leaders were touched by the lack of food. During previous times their skin was as white as snow, and their appearance shone as brightly as the luster of rubies. Now it is a different story, for now they are malnourished and appear no different from a common person of the street (verse 28).

Jeremiah believes those killed by the sword are better off than those who die by starvation. The death by sword is quicker, with less time to suffer. Those who starve die a slow and painful death. God is the One who poured out judgment upon the people in response to their sin. It is He whose fury has burned down Jerusalem.

This is the horrible picture of the pains the people experienced due to sin and rebellion toward God. There is a severe cost to anyone who lives contrary to the words of God and then stubbornly rejects God's call to repentance. God is true to His word. He fulfilled His promise to bring judgment upon the people by allowing His fiery wrath to consume the city.

One of the reasons the people of Zion grieved so much was for the loss of their country, because they were under the wrath of God. This point is not to inflict guilt upon anyone. However, the fact of God's wrath upon the people was because of their unrepentant, sinful behavior against holy God. Putting it plainly, we grieve because of the pain of God's holy anger against our sin. This was the situation of the people of Judah, and it is sometimes the reason for grief today.

Our grief often is the result of a self-inflicted choice. No one caused it but ourself, and God responds to our choice of sin by His punishment for our bad decision. This truth is found in various Scripture passages as follows: 1 Corinthians 11:29-32; James 5:14-16; 1 Corinthians 5:1-5; Romans 2:5; Numbers 32:23. Many Bible characters testify to the truth that God will show His just wrath upon unrepentant sin. David, Jonah, Ananias, and Sapphira are only a few examples that prove this point.

When God elects to pour out wrath that results in personal grief, it is for the purpose of manifesting His holy nature against our sinful action. He acts out of His nature of love in order to purify our life choices. J.I. Packer has defined God's wrath in the Bible as "never the capricious, self-indulgent, irritable, morally ignoble thing that human anger so often is. It is, instead, a right and necessary reaction to objective moral evil."[1]

We must understand that God is active in self-inflicted grief. As God deals with His wayward child, He does so for the purpose of teaching him to despise sin, and at the same time He seeks to draw him back into fellowship with Him. This is the value of discipline. The redeeming factor allows the fallen Christian to return to God in a manner that turns the tragedy into triumph. God is at work bringing honor to Himself and good for His child.

There is needed participation on the part of the person who has taken a course different from what God desired. We must come before God with true confession for our sinful action and receive His forgiveness (1 John 1:9). We also need to seek forgiveness and reconciliation to those people we have hurt in our sinful choices. Our responsibility to mend broken fences and to rebuild personal relationships is as a healing process to our grieving minds. God's responsibility is to forgive and show mercy and grace to the repentant soul (3:32-33).

This act of confession and repentance is referred to in Lamentations 2:42 by Jeremiah, but there is no national repentance there as in Lamentations 4:12. Therefore, God's wrath is in motion against the people. Those who have caused God's wrath upon them must know God loves them too much to allow them to remain rebellious toward Him. He knows just the right amount of pressure to put upon people to move them back to Him. He has given us the pathway to renewed fellowship with Him through confession and repentance from our sin.

Our grief is used by God to show us the depth of our sin and the need to return to Him. God uses our grief to give us a point of identity with His Son. No innocent person has ever suffered loss as Christ did. Isaiah portrays Christ in Chapter 53 as the suffering servant and declares Him as a "man of sorrow" and "acquainted with grief" (verse 3). Throughout His earthly ministry He wept over the rebellious city of Jerusalem, at the grave of Lazarus, and during His ministry on earth

(Hebrews 5:7). He knew the loss of being rejected by foes, family, and friends. The apex of His sorrow was on the cross as He felt forsaken by His Father. All of these images of Christ suffering sorrow afford us a point to identify with Him.

We are never alone as we grieve. The Holy Spirit is our Comforter. He is present with us during the pain. Second Corinthians 1:3-4 says: "Blessed be the God and Father of our Lord Jesus Christ, the Father of mercies and God of all comfort, who comforts us in all our tribulation, that we may be able to comfort those who are in any trouble with the comfort with which we ourselves are comforted by God."

God often uses grief as a way to help us see that Christ Himself suffered greatly, and we identify with Him as we grieve. He is both our Savior and our example.

Allow me to mention one final way in which God is involved with our grief. He desires to build faith in us during those moments when we feel He is very far away from us, so we grieve. He still loves us and has promised His abiding presence with us (Hebrews 3:5). We can count on Him to be our constant companion as we grieve (John 14:16). Remember, His name is Immanuel, meaning "God with us." Therefore, as we grieve, we do so with the aid and within the presence of our Lord Jesus Christ. As we allow His Spirit to comfort us, His love cuddles us as His little children. He gives us peace that is far beyond our human understanding. His presence is what we must have to heal and move on through the grief process. He is attentive to us as we cry out to Him in our sorrow. He captures every tear and places it in a bottle. He is involved with our grief more than we realize.

As we saturate our minds with His love for us and His presence around us, we are able to grieve with hope. We have hope because Christ defeated death and robbed the grave of its power as He resurrected. We who identify with Christ through faith have the hope that upon the return of Christ, we will be caught up in resurrected bodies as He was (1 Thessalonians 4:13-18).

Not only is our hope active now in our life with Him, but we also have hope in a place called Heaven that is free from all the discomforts of life here on earth (Revelation 21:4-5). God is keenly aware of our present trials, and the future for His children is so amazing and so wonderful that the splendor of it will make our present suffering seem to count for naught (Romans 8:18).

According to verse 12, the people of Zion fell into the trap of relying upon past success to prevent a present and future catastrophe for their city. More than a century before Jeremiah wrote these words, God had defended Jerusalem from an attack by the Assyrians. The record of this historical event is detailed in 2 Kings 19:36-37. Therefore, history provided a base whereby they believed that no king, even one as mighty as Nebuchadnezzar, could penetrate the city and bring destruction and captivity. Also, the people believed that they had a special position with God; therefore, God would never allow a disaster in His city.

The pride of the past made the people feel self-sufficient and independent from God. This is a picture of false security. Their trust was in their wall of defense and their strength. God allows grief to remind us of our inability to be self-sufficient and independent from Him. Grief serves as a wake-up call and causes us to depend upon God and trust in His provisions to protect us. The wall that surrounded the city was not sufficient for protection, as the people quickly discovered.

Verses 13-20 provide for us more of the many reasons the city fell. The blame is pointed directly at the spiritual and political leadership of the nation. The priests and false prophets along with the kings of the earth (verses 12 and 13) were guilty of parading the sin of self-sufficiency. Their confidence lay in a misdirected trust in themselves rather than a reliance upon God and obedience to His love. The false prophets told lies to the people to make them think God would not punish His people. They were only political pawns to appease the people by not mentioning their sin and affording them an opportunity to repent (2:14).

Jeremiah 6:13-15 gives to us God's condemnation of the false prophets and wicked priests who led the people into a false sense of security. As a result of their fabricating lies of security and peace, many lost their lives in God's retribution. They were guilty of shedding innocent blood. Not only did God reveal those guilty of failing in their responsibility to speak God's truth, but the people also rose up to condemn the false priests. These false priests were dishonored and rejected as if they were plagued with leprosy. They were driven out of town because no one wanted to be associated with them. Rejection is the price they paid for perverting God's word before the people.

Another reason for God's judgment upon the people of Judah was their trust in someone other than God. Jeremiah records the background of verses 17-20 of Chapter 4 in Jeremiah 37:5-7. These verses serve as historical background for this event. The people of Jerusalem placed a hope in the Egyptian army to break the siege that Nebuchadnezzar's army had upon Jerusalem. However, the army of Egypt was driven away by Nebuchadnezzar's army. The hope of Zion faded. To make the situation more hopeless, no other country offered any help to Jerusalem. Neither was there any hope in their King Zedekiah. He was at best a selfish and unstable king who was only concerned with his safety and escape from the Babylonian stronghold. He was called "the Lord's anointed, the very life of our nation" (NLT). However, his presence offered no protection.

The three most influential forces of the land (e.g., prophet, priest and king) were failures in saving the people from God's judgment. The people placed their confidence in mankind instead of placing that trust in holy God. God almighty was the only source of true survival and security. Their bad choices serve as a good illustration for us of where our trust must be located. God must be the center of our trust, and no one or nothing must take His place of priority in our lives.

To place confidence in any person or thing is a very common practice today. This action is a grave error and can be a reason for losing hope in the healing process of grief. As I write, I am seeking to be kind and compassionate, while at the same time avoiding the error of the false prophets of Jeremiah's time, which was being completely honest. There is always the tendency of humanity to place people and things as top priority in our lives. The truth is that God alone deserves that honor. To have anything before God makes us an idolater, and we lose focus on the Lord, who demands undivided love and allegiance from us.

Many times, I have marriage partners profess their commitment to each other by such expressions as, "He (or she) is the love of my life, and I could not live without him (or her)." The same is often spoken of the love they have for a child, a job, a friend, a pet, etc. I wonder, Has that object become the absolute loyalty of their life? If so, we find ourselves in the same plight as those in Zion who had lost their first love and replaced their loyalty to God with other things. This does not mean that God will allow death to come to that which rivals Him. However, we must remember that God will not have a rival. God so decrees that we allow people and things into our lives, but His desire is that they be given second place to Him.

One of the benefits of grief is that we begin to see clearly what our priorities should be. We often realize that the people whom we trust and have elevated to a position that only belongs to God are only human beings who will disappoint and fail us in our time of need. These things we cling to will lack the ability to give us peace in our time of grief. Only God is constant. He never fails. God is the ultimate Healer and Helper as we move through the grief process. When we advance through the pain and look back in the rearview mirror of the journey, God has been the only One who was always present and steadfast.

Perhaps the grief we experience serves to remind us that every life is important. God places people and things in our lives for the purpose of making our lives better and more complete. No person is to be taken for granted. Therefore, when God allows us to cross paths with people, let us learn to appreciate them for the value they are and the individuality they offer to us.

One thing that surfaces in my thoughts as I have experienced the grief of having two grandchildren pass into heaven is that there is a supreme priority upon life. A little child I will never hold or see or hear on this earth left a hole in my heart. Life is precious. Grief has a way of reminding us of the importance of life.

Time is a great asset. In the time God has allotted us, we should find the opportunity to reassess the moments that afford us the freedom to invest our lives into others. Those opportunities that came, yet we found reason not to call or visit our loved one, can serve not as times to regret or place guilt upon ourselves. There is enough of that already. But they can remind us that time is extremely valuable. It is very important to use those opportunities to connect with people who are special to us. When a loved one is taken or an object of our affection is lost, we become more aware of the impact they made upon our lives. The old saying is true, "We don't miss the water till the well goes dry."

The closing verses in Chapter 4 give us an insight into the Jews twisted desire for revenge upon the Edomites. Their desire was for the Edomites (whom the Jews hated) to receive a full measure of retribution from God because of their involvement in the destruction of Jerusalem. The people of Judah thought they had been punished enough (verse 22). Now they wanted wrath upon their enemies.

The Edomites are told to "rejoice and be glad" for the time being, but their time for God's judgment would fall upon them. Edom would soon be reduced to drunkenness and lewdness. Soon Judah's punishment would cease because her sins had been atoned for. Edom's sin would soon be judged, and nothing could be more hopeful for Judah. This vengeful hope is foreign to the teachings of Christ.

Two truths become apparent in verses 21 and 22. Number 1: God never gave up on Judah, and He will never give up on us. Number 2: There was hope in Judah of a day when the trials and suffering would end. Even though they desired punishment upon Edom, they believed in an end to their suffering and destruction. There is reason for us to have hope during our grief, too. There is great comfort in knowing that God is constantly at work in our lives through grief. We probably do not realize the handiwork of God during this time, but He is the Master Builder of our lives. He takes both good and bad experiences, weaves them together, and makes our lives beautiful according to His design.

There is a proverbial statement that says, "You can't make a silk purse out of a sow's ear." The meaning of this expression is that there is a limit to what you can do with the material that is available to you. Well, what is impossible to man is possible to God. As a result of His craftsmanship in our grief, He constructs amazing characters out of broken and damaged material. He has the touch to take broken hearts, wounded spirits, and hopeless people and shape their pain into a work of art for their good and His glory. Never underestimate what He will use or who He will use to create something new out of your grief-filled life. Michelangelo was asked by an onlooker what he was doing as he chipped away at a huge rock. Michelangelo responded by saying, "I am releasing the angel that is imprisoned in the marble." This is the greatness of our Lord's work in our lives. He releases the greatness of every person through their grief and hurt. Our Lord looks and sees us as we are, but He also sees the possibility of what we can become.

God used the suffering of Judah in such a powerful way that they never again worshipped idols. They were forever changed into a monotheistic nation who knew only one God: Jehovah. They were changed as a result of the captivity and destruction of their beloved city Jerusalem. The people of Judah had forgotten God's covenant with them, but God had not forgotten His promise to them. His judgment upon them was a harsh reminder that He would maintain His claim upon them even if He must send grief into their lives. God uses the harshness of loss to change us for His good purpose.

Having a firm grasp that God never gave up on Judah and will never give up on us helps us receive the second truth. The second glaring truth found in verses 21 and 22 is that of hope that Judah would rise to beauty once again and that her punishment would end (verse 22). Hope that is based upon God's word is inspiring and powerful and helps get us beyond being stuck in the darkness of grief. It gives us the promise that our circumstances will change, and that the winter of grief soon will turn to spring of life and newness. Joni Eareckson Tada describes hope by saying, "The best we can hope for in this life is a knothole peek at the shining realities ahead. Yet a glimpse is enough. It's enough to convince our hearts that whatever sufferings and sorrows currently assail us aren't worthy of comparison to that which waits over the horizon."[2]

There is an intriguing story that expresses hope that is solely based upon God's word. The story involves Jeremiah during a national crisis that offered no hope (Jeremiah 32). The Babylonian army surrounded Jerusalem and very soon the city would fall into their possession. God told Jeremiah that he should purchase some real estate in the town of Anathoth, which was Jeremiah's hometown. Jeremiah knew that soon the property would be of little value because the Babylonians would eventually control it. I'm sure Jeremiah offered up to God excuses for not purchasing the property. He probably recited the phrase, "Location,

Location, Location." However, God told Jeremiah to buy the property because someday God would bless the nation of Israel again. No savvy real estate agent would buy property that would soon be worthless. Well, Jeremiah trusts God's word and wisdom. He acts out of hope and buys the property. The action of Jeremiah is an expression of how the grieving person lives with hope, not by examining the circumstances, but by trusting in God's word for his life.

Our hope in God during the crisis of grief is not a hit-or-miss proposition, but a confidence in God's word to us. Our hope is more than an optimistic opinion. We hope in a way that expresses our faith in God and wait with assurance upon God to bring to pass in our circumstances what He has promised to us. There are times when all we have is God's word — and that is enough.

NOTES

1. J.I Packer, *Knowing God* (Dowvers Grove: InterVarsity Press, 1973), 151.

2. Joni and Friends Blog, "Encouraging Words for People Affected by Disability," April 23, 2018, https://www.joniandfriends.org/encouraging-words-disability.

Chapter 5
Prayer and Grief

Chapter 5 of this manual on grief is different from the previous four chapters. I will briefly mention these differences. Jeremiah writes this final chapter without the acrostic form. This is the only chapter in which Jeremiah does not employ this form of writing. For a more detailed writing style of Chapter 5, I suggest the wonderful book by Walter C. Kaiser entitled *A Biblical Approach to Personal Suffering*. It is not my purpose to explore the style of writing of Jeremiah. Once again, my purpose is to understand grief as it is expressed through the Book of Lamentations, and for those who grieve to find hope in the person of Jesus Christ.

Another difference in Chapter 5 from the previous four chapters is that this chapter is a prayer for the nation. It is not a lament as previous chapters. This is clear from the way Jeremiah is attempting to conclude his writing. Chapters 1, 2 and 3 have as their conclusion a prayer (1:20-22, 2:20-22, 3:58-66). However, Chapter 4 does not end in a prayer. Therefore, Chapter 5 is the prayer. This concludes Jeremiah's lament for his nation.

This chapter easily can be broken into two distinct parts. Verses 1-18 feature Jeremiah's description of the ruin of Jerusalem. Verses 19-22 are Jeremiah's petition for the renewal of Jerusalem. Let's listen to the great prophet Jeremiah as he prays for his nation.

Verses 1-18 speak to God and ask that God not forget the suffering of His people, but rather that He be quick to help relieve them from their plight.

Verses 1-13 review the humiliation and suffering the people have endured. Their property had been in their family for years, but now it is in the possession of the invaders. The price for basic needs in life is inflated to the point that the people go without. This is especially hard for the orphans and widows. Verses 6 and 7 are references to the past generation making covenants with pagan nations just to survive. Jeremiah sees this as a sin because such covenants between Israel and non-Jews were prohibited (Deuteronomy 7:2). This covenant-making expresses a lack of trust in God's ability to supply their needs, so they placed their trust in people rather than God (Jeremiah 2:18).

Verse 7 develops a thought that deserves some attention. Jeremiah writes, "Our fathers sinned and are no more, but we bear their iniquities." This is an earlier idea expressed in Jeremiah 31:29 and is an old proverb, "The fathers have eaten sour grapes, and the children's teeth are set on edge." The question often is asked by those who suffer, "Am I suffering from the sins of my ancestors?" Before one rushes to a quick answer, it's important to search more background Scripture.

A more thorough reading in Jeremiah 31:30 gives us the answer to the old wives' tale of yesteryear. Jeremiah is in full support of the truth Moses wrote of in Deuteronomy 24:16. The people of Judah were proclaiming this trite proverb as a way to place blame on the previous generation in order to escape ownership of their offenses to God. However, they had no solid theological ground to do so. Transferring blame does not clear one from his personal guilt. The harsh truth is that the present generation had sinned greater than the previous generations (Jeremiah 16:12). As one ponders the idea of generational sin, it is very important that the just character of God is stressed. Every person is accountable for his sin and no one else's. To play the victim in this context is to accuse God of unfair treatment. There is no excuse for personal sin as we try to place the blame on someone else. Part of being mature is assuming the responsibility for our actions.

Jeremiah bemoans the fact that life has reversed to the degree that those who were once slaves now are their masters. One can only imagine that the former slaves will show no mercy to their former owners (verse 8). These slaves who ruled over the people of Judah were actually Jews who were hired to inform the Babylonians of the language and customs of the Jews. They "sold out" to the opposition for the purpose of personal gain and preservation. These slaves were no more than thugs who often mistreated fellow Jews for the momentary thrill of being "superior" to those who suffered during this invasion.

There was an ongoing famine among the people that created a danger in their search for food. This famine was due to the army of Babylonia surrounding the city, and the gardens of the people of Judah became the property of the invaders. The Babylonian soldiers dished out harsh treatment to anyone who would venture out to find food. The people of Judah's skin dried and held tightly to their bones due to dehydration (verses 9 and 10).

Verses 11-18 are real stories of the humiliation the people of Judah faced. Their young maidens and women were abused sexually by the brutes who occupied the city. Their princes were publicly degraded by being hung by their hands for public display. Young men and boys were forced into slavery, grinding at the millstones. Among the city gates the elders who once gathered to talk or transact business were absent. Young men who expressed joy in their music were dancing in silence for their joy was gone. In the closing words of this paragraph, Jeremiah expresses the sadness in such a poetic way as he writes, "The crown has fallen from our head." We are hurting in our hearts and tears fill our eyes because of our sin. Our once beautiful city is so empty that only wild animals roam the streets (author's paraphrase).

Verse 16 expresses the end of the Davidic dynasty in figurative language.[1] The position of honor and respect had fallen. The dignity that Judah once wore as a result of the legacy of David has fallen into the dust of disgrace and shame, and the residents of the city felt this great loss.

The city that once was the queen of all others is now wasting away. Her temple was no more than a pile of rubble that only afforded a place for jackals to roam. The beauty was gone. What a sad picture of the results of sin (verse 18).

One cannot help but feel with this grieving prophet. To have seen such a prominent city and people now be reduced to shambles and ruination led to a great heartbreak and loss.

Perhaps there is a spiritual lesson for us to learn. Anyone who reads the words of this grieving, brokenhearted man knows that Jeremiah has poured out his soul to God and to his readers. He has been completely transparent in his attempt to express himself as he passed through several emotions. He has been real. He has said all he can say to his city and to God. He has emptied himself of his feeling of inner pain and grief. The city is in shambles and so are the lives of the people. There is nothing else to say or do, except pray.

With all honesty, many of us have reached that place where there seems to be no escape from the darkness of sorrow and grief. The dark clouds will not move from over our heads. We no longer believe that "tomorrow will be better." We reach a place that our hope in God, expressed by our prayers, is our only resource. When we reach the end of ourselves, we may discover a new beginning of confidence and hope in God. Often in our grief we discover that all we have is God. However, that's not the last of our discoveries. The greatest discovery is when we understand that He is enough for us to hope and place our faith in.

Chapter 5 reveals a very important weapon in our struggle against enslaving grief. Prayer is, without a doubt, a very important tool that assists us in dealing with our loss. This final chapter is one of prayer to God for Him to restore His people to their spiritual position before their fall into idolatry (verse 21). Certainly, the prayer deals with the restoration of their properties. But the thrust of the prophet's desire is for their repentance to God and a return to Him. Personally, I believe this chapter ends in a prayer because Jeremiah had exhausted every avenue to convince the people to return to God. The people rejected God's word. They chose to listen to the popular words of false prophets who only said what the people desired to hear. Yet no one repents from Jeremiah's preaching. He was persecuted by the officials and ridiculed by the people. Yet, he continued to warn of the coming wrath of God. The wrath did come as Jeremiah said it would. He did all he could and now he offers his prayer in the final chapter of Lamentations.

My point is brief yet true. Sometimes we can do all the positive things to push through the grief. We can consult the professionals and follow their orders. We can seek wisdom of our pastors and friends. We can work on reprogramming our minds to see things from a more positive point of view. Yet, sometimes we simply do not find a solution to the grief, and the only peace, hope, and restoration we find is in our time before God in prayer. Prayer must always be our first response and not our last resort. I, therefore, would never suggest putting personal attempts to get through grief before our personal encounter before God.

There are times in the grief process when we have tried all we know to do on a human level, and we have reached the end of our effort only to realize we are not healed. Then we discover that in the presence of Jesus through prayer, we find the greatest healing and comfort. In His presence we find the greatest security and peace. Second Corinthians 12:10 is the Apostle Paul's testimony of reaching the end of himself. He discovered his weakness and hardships only to see a great strength, not in himself but in God. Prayer gets us out of the confines of our weakness and connects us with the mighty works of God.

As I write these words, I grieve for my mother, who is suffering with Alzheimer's disease. I have watched a once active, healthy, and kind lady change into a person who now sits for long periods of time, who shakes during her waking hours, and who cannot remember how to get from one room to another, though she has made the journey many times. Her kind words and deeds of yesterday are gone and are only a memory to me.

Doctors have given us the diagnosis as well as a description for the end of life. There is no cure. The verdict is final. There is no chance that she will get better in time. The very best that my sister and I can offer is to make sure her last days with us are comfortable, and her needs are met. My hands are tied as far as giving her mind back to her. I cannot make her remember my wife's name or the names of her grandchildren. Those days are gone no matter how much I would like for them to return even if only for an hour.

What am I going to do when I can do no more? I am losing my mom on a daily basis, and I grieve. Feeling ill-equipped and insufficient to do anything is not a terrible place to be in our grief. Sometimes grief is a directional arrow that points us to a power higher than ourselves. In other words, God should be our focal point. He is our safe place, our peace, and our provider. We come to the limits of our self, our abilities, our knowledge, and our strength when our fuel tanks are empty, so we must look beyond our selves for additional help. The truth is that when we reach the point in our lives that we can only turn to God, we will soon realize that He is sufficient for our inadequacies.

Prayer is our connection to God. When we have done all we can, yet there is still much to be done, we feel helpless. This is our invitation to seek God's presence in prayer. In times of grief, sometimes prayer is all we can do to find comfort. Prayer is a communication with the living God that affords us a place of comfort and well-being. It affords us a safe place, if you will, before an omnipotent God who loves and understands us. Prayer releases us from our inabilities, so we find confidence in His abilities. He is our place of rest; something our grieving hearts need when we hurt.

This was what Jeremiah found to be true as he wrote Chapter 5. After reaching the place of pleading with the people to return to God and pleading with God to protect His people, only to see the stubbornness of the people and the judgment of God upon them, Jeremiah could do no more from a physical strength. He could only pray. That is what he does in Chapter 5.

I cannot say that prayer will reverse the disease of Alzheimer's (of course, that is possible with God), any more than God reversed His decision to bring Israel under judgment. What I can claim is that God will give us a supernatural strength, a wisdom, and a comfort during the losses in our lives. He may or may not choose to heal or bring back our losses. That is left up to His sovereign will. What is most important is that He might not change your circumstances but, in His presence, as you and I pray, He will change us. He gives us wisdom to see things from His perspective. He gives us sufficient grace to accept what we cannot change. He offers His peace through His abiding presence and those spiritual gifts from God are lasting for we never grieve their loss. Perhaps we never would have found His peace, His loving actions toward us, and His sufficiency if we had not reached the end of ourselves and turned to Him in prayer. Those unseen and inward gifts from God supersede all our moments of grief, and they are discovered through a prayerful relationship with God.

Prayer alters our mindset. As we pray, we are consciously or subconsciously admitting our need before God. We bow our heads and bow our knees as an act of submission. This physical outward act on our part says I admit my need, my inability to meet my need, and my dependence upon God to meet my need. The act of bowing in prayer is not necessarily a part of prayer. It is only a symbol of our submission and surrender to God.

As we admit our weakness and submit to God in due time, we begin to give up our notions that our personal agendas are better than God's. We do not plan to lose people, yet when life changes and people leave us through various ways, it often destroys our plans. We are confused as to the ways of God. Prayerful encounters with God teach us that His wisdom is far greater than ours. He shows us that we only know the past and some of the present, but He has full knowledge of all things. He teaches us that His wisdom is better than ours. My dreams are always subject to His will. The quicker I can accept this truth, the easier it is for me to move forward in my grief.

God teaches us through prayer that He can be trusted. He remains the anchor of our life when we grieve. Often as we grieve and pray, there is very little physical evidence that He is moving in our situation to diminish the pain. There is the temptation to stop praying and trusting for we see no sign of help. However, I urge you to press on in your prayerfulness and faithfulness. God is always at work, and one day when you pass through the darkness, you will review your journey and realize that God's constant help and sustaining presence was there at every twist and turn of your experience. God can be trusted, and prayer teaches this truth.

Being in the presence of God as we pray assures us of the confidence we gain in God's wisdom rather than our wisdom. Of course, when we lose something or someone precious to us, we question God's wisdom over ours. We are hurt. We wonder silently, if not audibly, if God made a mistake by permitting our loss. We ask many questions. We cast a lot of blame. We might express ourself in anger. All these reactions to our grief are normal. However, in prayer and over time, God settles our minds in His peaceful presence. Soon, we realize that we move from questioning His wisdom to confidence in His wisdom.

The stark reality in life is that sometimes there are no answers to our hardest questions. "Why did my mate die so soon?" or "Why did my friend linger in his pain?" I am not sure that if we did receive an answer to our many questions that one would satisfy us in our grief. There would just be more follow-up questions, and we would remain in the darkness of the unknown. God does not owe us any answers (Deuteronomy 29:29). He does not need our permission or acceptance of His will. He certainly does not need our approval to allow Him to work in ways that we deem unfair or unbeneficial to us. His ways will always be beyond our level of understanding, but not beyond our level of acceptance.

Too much energy is expended when we focus only on seeking answers. That time is better spent in just trusting in His perfect wisdom to do what is for His glory and our good. As we arrive at the place of accepting His work in the light of Romans 8:28, "And we know that all things work together for good to those who love God, to those who are called according to His purpose," we no longer seek for answers, but we come to trust that His work in us will prove to be spiritually beneficial for us. This acceptance continues to take us along the road to move beyond paralyzing grief. In other words, healing takes place when we stop searching for all the answers and start trusting in His works.

As we begin to accept the ways of God in our grief, we will continue to seek God's wisdom, but the form of our approaching God in prayer will change. The "why" questions turn to "what" questions: What are You teaching me as a result of my grief? What do You want to do in my life as a result of my grief? Another form of question might be in the "how approach." How do You want to use my experience in grief to help others? How will You be honored in my grief? These are healing questions that have answers that will develop us as persons of faith.

In reviewing Jeremiah's prayer in Lamentations Chapter 5, there are more lessons than I can give as to the value of prayer. However, there is one that needs to be mentioned before another subject is discussed. I have this mental picture of this deeply discouraged and depressed old prophet standing in his beloved city on a pile of rubbish, pleading with God. All around him are the ruins of a fallen city that at one time was a beautiful city, the envy of the known world. All that is left of Jerusalem are memories and destruction, and there, the man of God cries out to God. That is all he can do. His passionate preaching has fallen on deaf ears. He has done everything he can do, and now he directs his pleas to heaven, as he has often done before.

Jeremiah provides a good example for us regarding the consistency of prayer. Jeremiah had no real reason to continue to pray. God had destroyed the city. God's judgment had taken so many people and items that Jeremiah loved. Jeremiah had loved, lost, and now he grieved. However, Jeremiah continued to trust God. We know because he continued to pray. Jeremiah was very much human, and there were times he wanted to quit, yet he remained faithful. His prayerful desire was that the people would repent so that God's judgment would not come upon the city. That prayer was not answered. However, Jeremiah did not quit praying to God with unswerving faith.

Jesus taught us to pray and not faint (Luke 18:1). Jesus knew that the heart of humanity would give way to discouragement when prayers were not quickly answered. There is the tendency to give up if results are not seen within a short period of time. So, our Lord gives us encouragement in those times when we "faint" in our prayer lives.

We are to be relentless in our endeavor to pray even if results are not experienced when we think they should be. Don't quit in praying for a work of God too soon. It is always too soon to quit. God will always answer. He might say yes, and you hear from Him almost immediately. Sometimes God says no, and that is His answer. Learn to accept that He says no for your own good as His child. By the way, He said no to some of His greatest servants so, when He tells us no, we are in good company (Moses, David, Paul, and Jesus are just a few who had their prayer requests denied by God). There are times that God says, "Wait awhile. Now is not the right time for you to have this request in your life." Again, trust God's timing and rejoice that He knows what is best for you and what will glorify Him the most. Jeremiah serves as a great example because he did not "faint" in his prayer life, even when he saw no positive results from God.

We can learn much from Jeremiah concerning prayer. The exercise of prayer is more than getting our wish list filled by God. Prayer is more than making life free from pain and trouble. Prayer is an experience with God whereby we fellowship with God. Rather than trying to get something from God in prayer, we give our worship, adoration, praise, and service to Him. Prayer allows us to express our dependence upon Him as we ask Him for our daily bread. Our submission is expressed if we submit to His will being done and not ours. Prayer is not meant to make God our servant or our Santa Claus. Prayer is not wrestling with God to obtain our desires, or presenting our Christmas list to Him, or demanding that He jump at our every request. Our aim must always be "according to His will, not ours." Jeremiah realized that one day the broken lives and city would rise from the ruins. Jeremiah would never live to see it, but he knew the word of God, and Jeremiah prayed in faith that God's raising the city would come about. In that hope, Jeremiah would have an opportunity to praise and celebrate God for His perfect work.

My grieving friend, do not "cave in" to the pull of Satan to stop praying. God in His time and in His perfect way will act to bless you with the strength to move forward in healing from your broken heart. God is faithful. He is constantly at work in our lives to fulfill His wonderful purpose. Keep faithfully conversing with God — for when we do, He is well pleased.

In the midst of grief, the one element that keeps people moving forward in life is that of hope. Hope is the answer for how one goes on in life without a mate, a child, or a friend. Hope gives us a renewed interest in life as we focus on returning to a daily routine. Hope is what releases us from the paralysis of grief. Hope is the fuel for tomorrow.

Questions:

What is biblical hope?
How does it help me in the period of grief?
How can I have hope in the midst of hopelessness?

Foundation of Hope — Trust in God!

Thus far in the study of Chapter 5, I cannot help but feel as though there is a heavy black cloud that hangs over the prophet and the people. The dense cloud that appeared in Chapter 1 has lingered to the last chapter of this book of laments. Since this cloud has been apparent throughout these chapters and is an accompanying nemesis to those who grieve, it deserves a name. Hopelessness is its name. It invades every hurting and grieving heart unless it is met with biblical hope.

Hopelessness is an emotional state of mind whereby a person sees life as having no escape from a painful situation. If this thought pattern is not corrected, they believe there is little value or purpose to live. This is a state of mind when an individual can become so overwhelmed with the obstacles and difficulties of life that they believe they are too inadequate to overcome them.

Hopelessness is a dreary, dark, and lifeless place where the hurting go when lostness overwhelms their perspective of life. Hopelessness is a thief that robs a person's heart of joy and security. Hopelessness is a murderer, for it kills one's motivation to live. Hopelessness is a task master, for it enslaves the heart to depression and negativity in life. Hopelessness is a heavy weight that rests upon your chest to hinder your breathing and eventually starves you from breath. Hopelessness is like a road that leads into a dark place but never leads through it. On and on many images can be drawn, but none ever touches the depth of hopelessness that is in the soul of a person who has lost so much that they grieve to the point of total despair.

I remember reading the words, "People can live weeks without food, days without water, minutes without oxygen, but not a moment without hope." The number of suicides in the United States will attest to this statement's truth. From Wikipedia:

> Suicide is a major national social issue in the United States. In 2018, there were 48,344 suicides, up from 42,773 in 2014, according to the CDC's National Center for Health Statistics (NCHS). On average, adjusted for age, the annual U.S. suicide rate increased 24 percent between 1999 and 2014 from 10.5 to 13.0 suicides per 100,000 people, the highest rate recorded in 28 years. Due to the stigma surrounding suicide, it is suspected that it generally is underreported.[2]

Those who become hopeless due to grief must make proactive choices that will empower them to push through the feeling of hopelessness. Here are a few suggestions that will defend against the feelings of hopelessness. The way to deal with hopelessness should be divided into two major areas: Prevention and Preservation. The primary area of concern is learning what measures one should take to prevent the hopelessness. This is the first line of defense against hopelessness — prevent it from entering our hearts.

In order to prevent hopelessness from taking root in us, the following suggestions are offered:

Make certain your spiritual and emotional well-being are priorities in your life. Humans are made up of three vital parts that must be maintained on a consistent basis. These three parts are spirit, body and mind, and are so closely related that if one part becomes dysfunctional, the other two will follow. These three parts of the human soul form the wholeness of life. These three parts must be carefully balanced, and if not, life will be thrown out of the proper rhythm. That life that becomes out of balance is susceptible to many diseases of the spirit, body and mind.

First, we must give attention to our spiritual well-being. We should strive to maintain a close relationship with God. Spend time developing your spiritual life by a daily consumption of Scripture verses. Talk to God through prayer. Develop friendships with people who are on the journey of faith with you. This is accomplished by church and small group attendance. As previously mentioned, God is our Great Physician. He made us, and He is our healer.

Second, the physical side must be attended to as well. Eat moderately and make healthy food selections. Take time for yourself as you balance rest, work, and recreation. Take walks or cycle for excellent forms of exercise. You might join a fitness club so that you can associate with others as you take care of your physical needs. You alone know what you need at any given time. You may need to get up and move about, or you may need to rest and reflect on where you are in your progress with preventing hopelessness in your life.

Third, the emotional/mental side is the last part of the human soul that must be properly maintained. In order to prevent the darkness of losing hope and feeling life is not worth living, we must also give much attention to our thoughts.

Another way one can rise above the dark cloud of hopelessness is learning how to change our perspective on how we understand life's circumstances. We must remember the power of our mind. God has wonderfully made us with the ability to think of only one thought at a time. Go ahead and try to think of two thoughts at the exact moment. You can't. See I told you. We have the power to choose what we will allow to take residence in our minds.

Yes, negative and hopeless thoughts do enter our mind, but we do not have to allow them to remain. The simple truth is that our thought life dictates how we respond to every situation we encounter. This certainly is true as we combat hopelessness in our minds. Learning to reprogram our thinking is a lifelong endeavor, a very good tool to help us persevere and push through. It begins with a willful choice to do so. Here are a few suggestions:

Reject negative thoughts. Such thoughts as "I have no purpose for living" must not be entertained. The truth is, everyone has a purpose in life. You are special to someone. You influence someone by your very existence. You are worthy of love not only to God, but also to others. Entertaining such a thought is negative and untrue. Examine the negative thought by asking yourself if this particular thought is true. Is it founded on what God's word says? Does the thought lift my emotional life or bring it down?

Now that negative thoughts have been rejected, begin the process of putting a new pattern of thoughts in your mind. This step is of utmost importance. Here, you again must control your thought life. You are in command of your mind so command your thoughts to be more positive, truthful, and healthy. A wonderful illustration of this truth is found in Psalm 42:5, 11: "Why are you cast down, O my soul? And why are you disquieted within me?" Verse 11 repeats verse 5.

I believe there are some very important lessons to learn as we try to reorder our thinking.

The lesson is learning to talk to one's self, rather than listening to the opinions of others, as the psalmist talked to himself in order to control and correct his mind. This allowed him to keep his mind from entertaining untrue thoughts. He asked himself thought provoking questions that caused self-examination and a search for truth. When we allow our minds to run at will, they will be fed with lies and negativity. When we are in control, we tell ourselves the truth and pose questions that demand truth for an answer.

The psalmist is willing to correct his thought pattern. Upon honest questioning of himself, he reordered his thoughts. He had no true reason to be discouraged so he chose to rise above it. He immediately refocused his thoughts upon giving praise and thanksgiving to God, which supernaturally elevated his emotional well-being. He reprogrammed his mind with the wonderful and precious truths of God's supreme value to him. His emotions were elevated by refocusing his thoughts upon God.

Sometimes when you feel overwhelmed by the weight of grief, it is wise to find a place of quietness and call yourself into order. Evaluate yourself with hard questions that force truth from your heart. Questions such as: Why do I feel so defeated? Are these feelings legitimate, helpful, positive, or negative? What are my greatest blessings in life? Think on the gifts God has afforded you, rather than what you do not have. Then with God's help, focus upon the wonderful loving character of God and allow Him to express His love to you. Tell Him of your thankfulness for His leadership in your life and His wisdom. Honor Him as you refocus upon His strength and ability to meet every need in your life.

Another way we can persevere through the enemy of hopelessness is to agree with the inner emotion, but not accept it as the final verdict. To deny your feelings of grief, hopelessness, anger, despair, and denial is not being honest with yourself and will not advance your progress of healing. So, instead of rejecting these feelings, accept them. Admit these feelings are real, and then argue against their permanent residence in your mind.

The thought might enter your mind that your present situation is hopeless because the person you loved so deeply is gone. This is a statement that is often uttered in the moment of grief. That seems to be a true statement if someone is utterly hopeless. But is it really true? No, because we are individuals with an individual purpose for life. Although the feeling is real, it must be argued against, and an additional statement must be added, such as "I have lost the love of my life, but I must move forward in life and fulfill my life's purpose." Those who feel negative emotions during the grief period may face a common temptation. The temptation is to become a hermit and exclude people from their lives. This is confirmed by thoughts such as "I'm single again and I do not fit in with couples," or "I would only be a third wheel, so I'll just stay behind." Again, the thoughts are real, but not always true. There is a difference. Instead of denying the thoughts, honor them with some add-on statements (e.g., "I am single again, but being with other people is helpful to me," or "Although I am a widow, I am going out with some friends for an evening of fun and to be in the company of people"). Actually, there are many couples who would see entertaining a grieving person as an opportunity to help him through his loneliness.

One of the overlooked periods of grief is the loss of a pet. Often the response from the pet owner is, I will never have another pet because it hurts too much when I lose them. As one who has also felt the harsh sting of that type of loss, I can attest to that feeling for it is very real. However, it may not be the best decision one can make. Those of us who have loved and lost pets know life is better with an animal we can love, care for, and find companionship with. Therefore, we should not allow our feelings to keep us from the joy of another pet. There is great fulfillment in allowing a pet to rescue us (rather than the pet being rescued).

In order to push on through the hopelessness, we must focus on the hope we have for the future. When we understand that our future is much brighter than the feelings of despair that agonize our hearts as a result of hopelessness.

The intentional act of changing one's thought life is biblically sound (Romans 12:2 and Philippians 4:8-9) and is now supported by medical studies. Neuroplasticity is defined in medical dictionaries as: "The brain's ability to reorganize itself by forming new neural connections throughout life. Neuroplasticity allows the nerve cells (neurons) in the brain to compensate for injury and disease and to adjust their activities in response to new situations or to changes in their environment."[3]

Dr. Dennis Charney is the dean of Mt. Sinai School of Medicine, and he has studied how the brain responds in dramatic changes to people's environments. Dr. Charney describes how prisoners of war who were placed in solitary confinement developed unusual cognitive capacities because the only activity they were allowed to do was think. The POWs were exercising their brains. Dr. Charney is using this research to conduct psychological theories that can improve learning and memory and help solve problems dealing with anxiety and depression.[4]

The simple point is that as the grieving person learns to persevere through the cloud of hopelessness. He must know that the medical community gives credibility to the Bible that the brain can be re-nerved, retrained, or reprogrammed to think positive and truthful thoughts that takes one's emotions high above the cloud level of hopelessness.

This action takes time, patience, and prayer. This change in our minds will not come quickly or easily, but by the grace of God and great effort, our minds can be set above all that troubles us here on earth.

The last paragraph of this study is found in Chapter 5, verses 19-22. These verses are Jeremiah's pleaful prayer for God to restore the people. Within this section of Scripture Jeremiah express his hope that God will restore them to their prior days of glory.

Verse 19 is a diamond in the dust of despair. The verse serves as a fountain of truth that expels all the hopelessness within the Book of Lamentations. It serves as an answer to all the woeful circumstances the people of Judah encountered. This wonderful verse gives the reader a theological lesson on the character of God because it presents God as sovereign, unchangeable, and eternal in nature. The people have lost so much in ways of earthly possessions. Their beloved city was in rubble and in the possession of the foreign invaders. However, God is still there, and He is the one stable factor in their lives. Through all the dust of the overthrow of the city, the prophet could see God remaining on His throne. The earthly temple was ransacked, but the heavenly temple was still intact.

Jeremiah writes with celebration and exaltation in his voice. He has expressed his low moments in verses 1-18. Now he rises to proclaim the majesty of God's eternal and sovereign rule.

As mentioned before, grief has its moments of lows and highs. Grief is like a loose bulb in a light socket. There are both moments of dimness and brightness in the heart. This verse is the brightest in Chapter 5 because it is the foundation people can establish hope upon. This is real hope! The wonderful truth is that even in the midst of the destruction of the city, God continued to be there for His people. When everything is lost, God is still there!

Jeremiah returned to a dismal point as he voiced a question in verse 20: "Why do You forget us forever, and forsake us for so long a time?"

Jeremiah questions God's steadfast love for the people. He continues this form of questioning in verse 22. Yet, in the middle of this line of questioning, he makes a prayerful plea to God for repentance and restoration. The words of verse 21 in the King James Version are as follows: "Turn thou us unto thee, O Lord, and we shall be turned; renew our days as of old." Jeremiah again expresses the antidote for the troubles of the people in Judah. It is repentance. This is a major theme throughout Jeremiah's writing. The call of Jeremiah is clear to repent by rejecting the old ways of idolatry and becoming centered upon God. Repentance, according to Jeremiah, means a turn of 180 degrees from sin to God. The people need to reject the old ways of idolatry and become centered upon God.[5] This entails a godly sorrow for sin that leads to personal repentance and results in a changed mind and action of lifestyle.

The sad truth was that the people rejected Jeremiah's message. They chose to continue headlong into sin and selfishness. Now the payment for their actions was due. God had not forsaken them, but rather the people had forsaken Him. Their only hope was in God, but they must return to Him in repentance.

Verse 22 is a statement that is negative: "Unless you have utterly rejected us, and are very angry with us!" Some understand this verse to be in the form of a question and is stated in such a way as to say that it is impossible for God to reject His people and to be constantly angry with them. Keil, in his writings on the *Prophecies of Jeremiah*, suggests that verse 22 is a continuation of verse 21 for restoration.[6] In reading the verse in the form of a question it seems to imply that hopelessness is inevitable. Without the question marks, the end of Lamentations is nothing but dread, rejection, and offers no chance of their prayer being answered. This is no helpful way to end the counsel of the God of all comfort.

Such a continual anger at His people is contrary to the nature of a loving God. God's promises for Judah's future were sure and unforgotten. God would perform for the people what He had promised, and they could be hopeful for that.

Verse 22 should be looked at as a question: For have You utterly rejected us? This is the question of the prophet on behalf of the people. Knowing the character of God, the response of Jeremiah is as follows, "And are very angry with us." Yes, God had shown His anger, but soon His anger will abate. In time, His promise would be fulfilled to Judah.

The book closes with a series of serious questions that reflect the anguish of the people as well as the recognition of the wonderful character of God. There is nothing wrong in asking questions. Our response to our grief is often that of questions — questions such as, "Why did this happen to me?" "Where is God in the midst of my loss?" "When will this grief go away?" These are normal reflections of our thought process and often express our inward pain. Throughout Scripture, people have asked questions. The psalmist, the disciples, and even Christ on the cross all expressed their inner emotions in the form of questions. The point is simply that it is all right to ask questions in times of grief.

The questions from the prophet had been answered in the earlier chapters of Lamentations. Chapter 5:20 asks, "Wherefore dost thou forget us for ever, and forsake us so long time?" (KJV). The answer is in Chapter 3, verses 21-25. The one prevailing answer to the suffering of the people is that the fault of this tragedy upon the people was due to their sin and neglect to repent to God. They made the choice to reject the message of repentance. Therefore, their payday has now arrived.

Perhaps at times when we ask questions, we might already know the answers, but we may not have accepted the answer. There are some questions in this life that have no answer that would satisfy us. Therefore, God chooses to remain silent. He knows we are tender during our grief, so He refuses to answer these questions. Maybe He will answer later by the way He orchestrates our lives. Delayed answers to our questions are good, too. Perhaps when we get to heaven, He will explain all the answers to our questions. However, when we get to heaven, the answers will not really be needed. The answers will not be important for all our questions will grow dim in comparison to His glory.

The answer to our questions may not be an explanation from God. The question or answer is not the objective. The objective is found in verse 19. It is clinging to the solid foundation of the character of God's sovereignty and immutability. It is knowing Him. From that comes our trust in Him, and that provides us with the hope we need in times of great grief.

As we develop a deeper understanding of God's nature, we serve ourselves better than seeking answers to questions that have no answers. We can put to rest many questions by a great trust in the nature of God.

In order for us to develop our knowledge of God's character, a brief listing of such identifying qualities will be a great help. There is much of God's character that we will never know. He is beyond our human wisdom, yet He has revealed enough of Himself through Jesus Christ, His Son, that we can anchor our thoughts to Him. He has chosen to show us Himself through the personality of Jesus. Here is a list of His attributes that He has revealed to us so our minds can have peace when we are filled with questions.

God is love (1 John 4:8) — His nature is love. All He does is from this character of love. God cannot abuse or mistreat humanity for His nature is that of love.

God is holy. He has no sin or flaw in His character. Therefore, all His works are from the nature of a pure being.

God is just (Deuteronomy 32:4) — God is fair. He will act out of justice.

God is righteous (Genesis 18:25) — Being of the nature of righteousness means He will always do right. His nature is the standard for right. He makes no mistakes. From our position of grief, we often consider ourselves victims of life's inequalities. However, from God's position, He is righteous and sovereign. He allows everything into our lives for a purpose, and He is always right as He does.

God's character is wrath. Because of His purity and holy nature, there must be the part that despises sin and its awful results. He will judge and punish all that is against His nature. God is slow to anger. He is patient and gives people time to repent. However, there is a time when the wrath of God reaches a point when it spills out upon sin and sinners.

There are many more attributes that are ascribed to God's nature. However, this writing will not explore them. Enough light has been shed to help us put together an elementary understanding of God so we can develop a trusting faith in His character and purpose for us. We can rest assured that God loves us, even when our feelings tell us otherwise. Out of His love for us, He will never abandon us and treat us as orphans. He is too good to be unkind and unjust to us, regardless of our circumstances.

There is another truth that is exposed in Chapter 5 that is very important in the grieving of our losses. As I ponder Jeremiah's prayer in Chapter 5, I sense there is a great hope that dwells in his heart, even when he sees hopelessness all around him. I think Jeremiah hopes God has not forgotten His people and will, in His timing, return His people to Himself and also heal their land (verse 19). Jeremiah did not see any physical evidence of God's action of restoration at the time of His prayer. However, hope does not have to see something to believe it eventually will happen.

There are many "tools" in God's spiritual toolbox that He makes available to us as we work through our grief. Without a doubt, biblical hope is one of those most valuable tools.

The word "hope" is used today in order to express a wish or a desire. For example, we say, "I hope my friend recovers from his surgery," or "I hope my team wins the Super Bowl." This is a hope that has no basis for certainty and is at best a 50/50 probability of occurring. These expressions offer the possibility that your friend may not recover from the surgery and that your team may not win the Super Bowl. Such a definition of hope in this usage is used in the secular vocabulary.

Biblical hope is not tainted with the possibility of failure. It is filled with certainty. Biblical hope is a confident expectation. Biblical hope is founded upon the character of God. God is truth; therefore, He cannot deceive us. Biblical hope is based on His word. Therefore, His promises are sure to us. As we read His holy word, we discover more of His character and His ways of dealing with people, especially those who need comfort. Because He and His word are steadfast and unchanging, God gives us confidence that His many promises do come true.

This hope is sure and unchanging. It is as solid as the character of God. This hope carries the grieving person through the dark nights of the soul until the light of a new day arrives. This hope enables the brokenhearted to push through their heaviness of heart. This hope is most precious to those who grieve for it enables them to see the unseen future through eyes of faith. This hope is the confident expectation that God will redeem our painful experiences, and at the end of the unpleasant experience in our lives, He will make all things new (Revelation 21:5). This biblical hope is placed in us by the Holy Spirit as we digest God's word in our hearts. This is supernatural hope that sustains us in every event in our lives. As we claim God's promise by faith, those promises become hope that keeps us looking forward to a better time and place in our lives. At the present time we may not see any evidence of a more pleasant future, but hope gives us confidence that our future is greater than our present and past.

How could this grieving prophet write of such enthusiastic hope? He had no human reason to do so. All he loved had been lost or taken over by a foreign army. Yet, Jeremiah is a beacon of hope in some of the most tragic of circumstances. The reason for Jeremiah's hope is the same as every believer's hope. He had heard from God. As stated earlier, God's word to us in the Bible is the foundation for hope. Jeremiah speaks of hope in the book that bears his name as well as in the Lamentations. A quick study of hope in his writings will help us understand how Jeremiah could be hopeful during the destruction of his beloved city.

Jeremiah recognized that God was "the hope of Israel." God was Israel's savior in times of distress (Jeremiah 14:8). This verse expresses a bit of sarcasm toward God, yet Jeremiah could not deny Him the title of "the Hope of Israel." This verse expresses a bit of irony. The people thought of God as a traveler simply passing through Israel and giving little thought of helping them in their plight. Yet, they knew that God was "the hope of Israel." Jeremiah 17:12-13a piggybacks on Jeremiah 14:8 and enlarges upon God as the "hope of Israel": "A glorious high throne from the beginning is the place of our sanctuary. O Lord, the hope of Israel, all who forsake You shall be ashamed."

Leo Green, in his excellent writing on Jeremiah, believes these verses refer to the transcendent being whose presence fills the universe. It is in God and Him alone that we find salvation and security. God is our hope and salvation in every situation.[7] This is the attitude of Jeremiah toward God. In Him, there is hope. Without Him, there is hopelessness (John 15:5).

Some of the most beautiful words that fell from the pen of Jeremiah are found in Jeremiah 29:11. These words cover our disturbed hearts like a warm blanket on a cold night. In our times of grief, there is often the feeling of bewilderment. We are confused as to where our grief is taking us, or what the emotional effects will be upon us. This verse is for every uncertain soul. Here is God's assurance to Israel. God knows. He knows His plan He has for His people. His plans are not to hurt them but to give them a "hopeful future." Hear these promising words with your heart: "For I know the plans I have for you, says the Lord. They are plans for good and not for disaster, to give you a future and a hope" (NLT).

Jeremiah held to hope in God for he knew God had a plan for His people.

The plan God has is mixed with His promise in Jeremiah 16:14-15. God's plan was to restore His people to the land of Israel. The judgment, destruction, and enslavement were only temporary. The plan was to restore His people unto Himself as He brought them out of Egyptian captivity. God's plan was unfailing, and this established hope in Jeremiah's heart.

Lamentations 5:19 is an expression of hope by the writer: "But Lord, you remain the same forever! Your throne continues from generation to generation" (NLT).

This verse is saturated with the sovereignty and steadfast eternal character of God. Those who are in the grip of grief need this consistency of God. They need someone to hold to while the foundation beneath their feet erodes. Their life needs stability. The truth of God that is as sure as the nature of God affords people hope. Our hope in God is based upon His excellent character. We can trust His promises. He will sustain us in hopelessness because of His eternal being. He will give us security as we stand in His presence and worship Him even if we must stand alone.

Jeremiah often mentions God's throne in his writings (see Jeremiah 3:17, 14:21, 17:12, 49:38, 52:32; Lamentations 5:19). From his writings, one can observe that Jeremiah had a very lofty idea of God's sovereignty and of God's nature. According to Jeremiah, God's reign is from everlasting to everlasting. Perhaps it was Jeremiah's words the Holy Spirit reminded John the revelator of as he wrote Revelation 19:6b: "Alleluia! For the Lord God Omnipotent reigns."

Jeremiah knew that God, under no circumstances, would renounce His people, renege on His promises, or relinquish His position as Sovereign. This is the substance that biblical hope is founded upon.

Up to this point, I have not mentioned any references from the New Testament that deal with hope, simply because the focus is upon the writings of the Old Testament prophet, Jeremiah. However, hope takes on flesh and reaches its apex in the person of Jesus Christ. He is the fulfillment of God's hope for all people. He is our hope today of an eternal life in the future. All that was prophesied in the Old Testament came true in the person of Jesus Christ. Without the redeeming Christ, grief would be an eternal wound. However, because of Christ's victory over death by His resurrection, grief for the believer will be temporary. His resurrection gives us hope that there is a transition for all Christians, and that our physical death is only a step into His presence forever.

Regardless of the depth of loss and grief, our God is unchanging in His desire to take us from a place of grief to a palace of glory. In the time span between our grief and glory, we should remain hopeful in His promises. These promises are supported by the greatness of His character. Did Jeremiah believe on this hope, or did he simply preach it to the people in order to give them encouragement in a harsh time? Everyone knows that high and lofty words sound good to say and to hear, but there is a great difference when life experiences challenge us to incorporate them into action. This question deserves an answer. We need to know if Jeremiah practiced what he preached. If not, we can see hope from a worldly stance, and we have no real proof that biblical hope exists. If so, we need to see that this great prophet really believed and acted on his trust of God's word.

There is an answer for our question, and it is revealed in Jeremiah 32. In the midst of very discouraging times, Jeremiah exercised a dynamic hope in God with a single action. Here is the story of Jeremiah putting into his life what he believed about God's word.

God spoke to Jeremiah and informed him that his cousin, Hanamel, would come to him and offer to sell his land in the town of Anathoth. Anathoth, as you know, was the hometown of Jeremiah, and by law Jeremiah being a family member had the right to buy the property before the land would be offered to the public. Just as God promised, Hanamel did come to Jeremiah and made an offer to sell.

For a moment, allow your mind to think about what Jeremiah did by purchasing the property. For 40 years, Jeremiah had proclaimed the fall of Jerusalem and the captivity of the people. He, of all people, knew the land would soon become the property of the Babylonians. Hanamel knew the time was right to sell his property so he would not lose it. He took the money and ran. Anyone who could see would know that the fall of Jerusalem was imminent. No wise investor would buy real estate knowing that the market would soon fall. However, Jeremiah is not your average worldly person because he has heard from God. Jeremiah expresses his hope in God as he purchases the property upon a word from God that the future is greater than the present. Jeremiah does not look at the circumstances, nor does he listen to those who see no future. He listens only to God because he knows God is true. Therefore, Jeremiah acts upon the word of God.

Jeremiah did not purchase the property because he wanted to keep it in the family, or because it would be a great investment, or even because of its "location, location, location." He bought it because God said to buy it. In other words, Jeremiah obeyed God. This action of

Jeremiah wonderfully illustrates what it means to have and express hope in a difficult time because hope is not founded on what is seen, but upon what God says. In verse 15, Jeremiah makes this tremendous faith statement: "For thus says the Lord of hosts, the God of Israel: Houses and fields and vineyards shall be possessed again in this land."

Jeremiah deserves much credibility for what he does. He puts into action his belief in God's word. He serves as an example for every one of us to do the same in our dark situations in life. He sets before us a pattern of exercising hope. He teaches us to put our focus on God and not upon our grief. He teaches us to look beyond our past and focus upon a more wonderful future. Jeremiah teaches us to stop seeking answers and start holding the promises of God. There is one more truth that is evident in Jeremiah 32. He teaches us to make an investment. There is little one can do about the hurts and losses of the past. There is much we can do to invest in the future. Someone has rightly said that the windshield of your car is larger than the rearview mirror for the purpose of looking forward, rather than looking backward. Through hope in an unchanging, promise-keeping, and loving God, we can move forward in life and discover that all along our journey God has always done His best for us.

NOTES

1. F.B. Huey Jr., *The New American Commentary* (Nashville: Broadman Press, 1993), 487.

2. https://en.wikipedia.org/wiki/Suicide_in_the_United_States.

3. William S. Shiel, MD, MedicineNet medical author, "Medical Definition of Neuroplasticity," https://www.medicinenet.com/neuroplasticity/definition.htm.

4. Daniel Honan, "Neuroplasticity: You Can Teach an Old Brain

New Tricks," https://bigthink.com/think-tank/brain-exercise.

5. Walter C. Kaiser, *A Biblical Approach to Personal Suffering* (Eugene: Wipf & Stock Publishers, 1980), 118.

6. C.F. Keil and F. Delitzsch, *The Prophecies of Jeremiah: Biblical Commentary on the Old Testament, Vol. 20* (Grand Rapids: Eerdmans, 1956), 454.

7. Leo Green, *The Broadman Bible Commentary, Vol. 6*, "Jeremiah – Daniel," (Nashville: Broadman Press, 1971), 103.

Conclusion

The conclusion of Lamentations ends as it began — with questions. These unanswered, thoughtful, hard questions still remain in Jeremiah's mind. To be completely honest, these pesky questions linger in our minds as well. Jeremiah leaves these questions hanging without an answer for a purpose. I think he teaches us that there is no quick fix to grief. There always will be unanswered questions. These unanswered questions during our grief run contrary to our desire to have an immediate solution to our concerns. We watch a two-hour movie where the plot exposes a deep problem, and before the movie is over, someone has made everything right and the end meets with applause. To have instant satisfaction after a short time of discomfort is what we expect, especially if we have prayed for positive results. This is the American perspective of how hurt is to be overcome — quickly, completely, and cost-effectively. This is not how the Book of Lamentations ends.

Actually, this is what we should learn by reading many of the miracles of Jesus. Not all, but the majority of His miracles had instant and complete results. We often expect the same as we seek an answer to our heartfelt prayers. We want a solution yesterday.

We should allow the Book of Lamentations to speak to us rather than read into it what we think Jeremiah says. One of the stories of Jesus with His disciples sticks out from the others because the ending of it is left up to the reader to interpret it from a personal perspective. The story is found in Matthew 17:27. Jesus tells Peter to satisfy the government officials by paying tax. To do so, he is to go to the lake, throw in a hook, and the first fish he catches will have a silver coin in its mouth. Jesus instructed him to use the coin to pay the tax. The assumption is that Peter obeyed and paid the required tax with the coin he pulled from the mouth of the fish. However, there is no biblical statement that Peter carried through with what Jesus said.

Although implied, the conclusion is written by the reader and made from how the reader understands the character of Christ. I am aware the point of this story is not the fish, tax, or the coin. The focus is upon the contrast between the free people of righteousness and those who are slaves to an earthly system.

The conclusion of Lamentations leaves me with this same type of interpretation. There is no immediate answer to the prophet's prayers for restoration. In fact, he ends his writing with questions for the reader to answer as we understand the character of God. Jeremiah concludes the way he began in Chapter 1 by begging God with a deep sense of anguish to rescue the people from their loss.

Grief as a result of loss always brings questions. This is natural for those who grieve. However, sometimes there are no answers. We have to rely always upon the ways and wisdom of an almighty God and trust in His character.

Throughout this writing, I have formed some conclusions for the ending of my personal laments in life. Even though Jeremiah's writing does not end in a fairy tale ending, such as "and they lived happily ever after," there are some conclusions I have drawn that help me to move from paralyzing grief to glory.

First, grief comes from many losses, and to every person, regardless of our position in life. No one is exempt from grief: Christian, non-Christian, male, female, rich, poor, educated, uneducated. We have been or will be grief's victims. Do not waste your energy thinking God is unfair to you or that you are above this experience. Put your effort into accepting the grief and seeking to grow from the experience.

Second, realize that the answers we expect might not come — ever. Put your focus upon God's faithful promises. Answers might change with time and emotions. God's promises are of His presence and love and nothing else. There will be moments when you think you are all alone, encased by four walls, where there are no exit signs, but remember that dead end you stand on is a rock called Jesus, and He is stable enough for you. In your darkness He is the light that will never go out. In your confusion when you cannot find an exit, remember He is the way.

Third, keep moving forward in your grief journey toward glory. Get to know the character of God better than you have ever known it. God is too wise to make mistakes; too loving to be unkind; too merciful to leave us alone without His word in our lives. Remember that this is a marathon and not a 100-yard dash. For many the journey will last the rest of their lives, but it is not in vain. Along the way, God is doing His work that will end one day, and if we will allow Him to work in our life, we will be so joyful due to the results.

The journey will move you from grief to grace. You and I cannot make this trip alone.

We need the grace of God to encourage and equip us to do so. Part of God's grace toward us is other people who are journeying with us. God puts them there because we need them or they need us. Learn to connect with people. Bless them and let them bless you.

Looking in the rearview mirror of my life as I make this trip from grief to glory has caused me to realize that all the moments of "successes" or "breakthroughs" that I thought I achieved have only been mirages in my desert of life. I now have a clear vision of a partner along with me who has cleared the way for my easy passage through grief. His name is Jesus, and by His grace I have traveled far to the place I am now. I do not claim to have recovered completely from my grief, but by His grace, He has done a good work in me. He will do the same for you.

As I write these last few words, I must say with glee that all my existence is summed up in one amazing word. It is called grace! His grace will lead me home.

Epilogue

I will never forget the date of October 21, 2019. The time was around 4:30 in the afternoon when my wife Barbara received a phone call that would forever change our lives. On the other end of the call, I recognized the frantic voice of my daughter, Diana. The words I heard her speak were so painfully devastating that they were engraved in my mind. Three single syllable words echo in my ears until this day. Diana said, "Jack is dead!"

Jack was my 11-week-old grandson and the son of Allan and Diana Williams. Suddenly time felt so surreal. How could this horrible news be true? I was with him the previous day. He looked so healthy and strong. He was fast asleep in his carrier. He was dressed in his new brown overalls. I looked at him with pride. He was a big boy (like me). He had a tint of red hair (like me when I was younger). I boasted that he looked like me (that is what grandparents are supposed to do).

Within minutes we were on our way to be with Allan and Diana. As we arrived at their home, we were met by two Hickory police officers. A yellow tape surrounded their house that declared the premises to be a crime scene: Once we identified ourselves as grandparents, the officers kindly directed us to where Allan and Diana were.

I drove less than one-half mile to find the road blocked off by a police car. I could see the red lights of an ambulance. I could see more eye-piercing blue lights from police cars. Once again, yellow tape told us of the seriousness of this situation. I identified myself to the police officer who blocked our entrance. I told him that we were the grandparents and our purpose was to be with Allen and Diana. He graciously allowed us to enter.

I rushed to Diana's side. She sat in her car stunned and almost in a state of shock. Words that describe her appearance were confused and puzzled. God allows us to enter into a numb state in order to protect our mental state as we grieve during traumatic experiences in our lives. As I reached out to hold her, a flood of tears rushed down my face. My deepest desire was to help my daughter escape from the reality that her infant son had gone to sleep and did not wake up. I felt so inadequate. There were no words, only sobs and groans would come out from the depths of my heart. I reached for Allan and I held my son-in-law, and only tears could I utter. He, too, was so broken by the death of his son. I could do nothing but hold Allan and Diana and cry with them as if tears had power to return Jack back into their arms.

There have been many losses in my life. As a pastor, I have ministered to many whose tragedies have caused me deep concern. However, none have rocked me to my core as the pain I saw in Jack's parents that fateful evening.

Jack's lifeless body was taken to the local hospital. We were informed that no one, including his parents, could see or hold him because of the ongoing investigation. This information caused a deeper wound in our hearts. However, more disturbing news would follow. We were told that an autopsy would be performed on his little body. Wave after wave of disconcerting information was simply too much for us to digest.

This is an excellent time to say that our family is very much aware of the responsibilities of law enforcement. We appreciate the professionalism that every first responder showed that day. We know that certain protocols must be performed, and we respect their profession. Yet, in that waiting room at the hospital, we felt so helpless. After much pleading, I was relieved that the medical examiner, the chief of police, and the nursing supervisor allowed Allan, Diana, both grandmothers, and my youngest daughter, Dedra, to view and hold Jack. I chose not to see him. I chose to remember him as I saw him the day before. We grieve differently. I chose to remain in the waiting area and pray for those who decided to see Jack.

I am forever grateful for the tremendous support that Allen and Diana received that night. Their friends in the community, their church family, and ministerial staff of Corinth Reformed Church became extensions of Jesus Christ to give love and emotional support to them. As friends gathered by their side and the waiting area filled with caring people, I found an opportunity to slip away from everyone and get my mind composed. I sat down on a curb just outside the hospital entrance and continued to weep in ways that I have never done before.

I never felt impressed to be strong for anyone. I did not have the energy to assume that role. Nor did I ask the age-old question of "why." At that time my broken mind would not understand any answer. All the questions would not bring Jack back. However, I did make some choices as I sat outside the hospital. The main choice I made was how I would grieve. I chose to grieve in such a way that would exemplify the hope that every Christian has found in the risen Christ. I will grieve as any grandfather would if they experienced the loss of a grandchild. I was determined to grieve with hope and to be an example of Christ in me (1 Thessalonians 4:13).

In order to grieve in a way to honor Christ, I had to make some choices that would help me reach that goal. Some of those decisions were made as I sat outside the hospital. Others were made later in the week. Those choices served as a GPS to help me navigate around the potholes of faithlessness. They helped me stay focused on the goal of grieving as one who has hope in God. Trust me — my choices are not some deep-blue theological mysteries that are secretive to everyone else. These commitments I made are available to anyone who seeks to move through grief to glory. Nor can I claim that my grief disappeared at Jack's funeral. I continue to grieve for my loss. These commitments continue to serve as navigational points that hold my life together in some of my darkest hours. I write of them in hopes that anyone who grieves can be confident that there are ways to move beyond grief to glorifying Christ.

My first commitment that helped me remain faithful is that I firmly believed that God is a good and loving heavenly father. I hold on to the truth that He is all wise, powerful, and involved with my loss and grief. There are two reasons for this belief: (1) The Bible tells of His love for me; (2) I know of His love because I have experienced it in the past. This anchor is foundational to everything else that I would choose to believe. I refused to doubt His love for me and my family.

The second commitment that kept me grounded in hope is the truth that God is the sovereign ruler over my life and destiny. I surrendered ownership of my life years ago. In fact, years before I had a wife, three daughters, three sons-in-law and grandchildren, I gave God full possession of myself and all future possessions. I gave all my life to Him because I know He is a sovereign loving Father. I can trust Him. I exist for Him. He does not exist for me. He has full freedom to allow circumstances into my life that are not very pleasant. He never has asked my permission for anything. Nor has He given me a copy of the blueprint that He uses to shape me into His likeness. My only choice is to submit to His will for my life.

Since God possesses and loves me, He has a plan for me. He

constantly is working out His plan in me. Jeremiah 29:11 was real to me long before it became popular. As precious as the verse is, I must confess that from my vantage point there are times that God's plan makes little or no sense. As I write, there seems to be no human reasoning for the death of Jack. He was, as far as I can tell, loved, healthy, happy, and a wonderful addition to our family. There is no purpose I see for Jack's death. I admit my understanding is very limited. However, God knows better and more complete than I do. His wisdom is far greater. His ways often are confusing to me, but He knows the way He goes (Isaiah 55:8-9).

To be honest, I am not certain that I will ever know the full plan of God as it concerns Jack's death. Maybe in heaven I will understand more completely. On second thought, the purpose will not matter because I will be so overwhelmed with the glory of Christ and seeing Jack that all my unanswered questions will vanish in the splendor of it all. For now, my faith resides in my heavenly father who loves me and is sovereign. My faith is in Him who is perfect in all His plans for me.

The third commitment that kept me focused on the goal of Christ honoring grief was to remind myself that just because I am a follower of Christ does not insulate me from loss and grief. I am afraid that prosperity preaching has led us to falsely believe that God wants His people to be healthy, wealthy, and anything less than that is the failure of your lack of faith.

Our friend in the Old Testament, whose name is Job, had a similar idea. He could not accept the idea of personal loss because he was a good and godly man. The notion that good people who serve God should prosper and evil people should suffer sounds good, unless you are grieving and godly at the same time. It simply is not true that God will keep sickness, sorrow, and death away if you serve Him. If you don't believe me, ask Paul the Apostle, Jeremiah, or multitudes who follow Christ in times of harsh persecution. If their testimonials do not convince you, then read the life and death of Jesus Christ. The unavoidable truth is that everyone is equal in the arena of loss and grief. The rain or sorrow falls on the just and unjust. When followers of Christ grieve, our focus should be that God always has a purpose for our loss. He never wastes our pain. He uses it to refine and mature us so He can use us for His will. As we seek to see beyond the immediate moment to the potentiality of our usefulness for the Kingdom of God, it helps us to know that God is not finished His work in us.

Unlike us, God uses broken things. He uses brokenhearted people. Grief breaks us from our personal confidences and self-reliance, so we are totally dependent upon His abilities, not ours. It is in the laboratory of life's loss and grief that we learn about the grace of our Lord. It is in the place of pain that our faith is tried, and He brings us out as refined silver.

Lastly, God helped me make another commitment that I held to that helped me as I grieved. God reminded me that He is not finished with me or our family. He brought to my mind Joel 2:25-26:

> *And I will restore to you the years that the locust hath eaten … . And ye shall eat in plenty, and be satisfied, and praise the name of the Lord your God, that hath dealt wondrously with you: and my people shall never be ashamed (KJV).*

During grief, it is important to remember that our great Shepherd restores our souls.

The truth is that our lives changed forever when Jack died. The Lord let our family "borrow" Jack for eleven weeks. The Lord gives and the Lord takes away. When God takes away, we grieve, but we do so by faith that He restores our souls with a deeper purpose and greater direction. There is absolutely nothing or no one who can replace Jack. He was unique, as is every person. I know of no member of our family who would want Jack to return to us. I am equally sure that if Jack were asked to come back, he would kindly refuse our invitation. How then will God restore to me what has been taken? Jack is not gone forever. One day I, too, will arrive in heaven and be reunited with him. Our separation is temporary.

The semi-colon is used in English literature to show a pause between two clauses. The semi-colon is stronger in purpose than a comma. In my mind I have placed a semi-colon after Jack's death. Now there is a temporary pause between his absence from us and my arrival in heaven.

I still believe in Easter. I hold firmly to the hope that is in the resurrected Christ. His promise to His children is that not only will we suffer as He did, but we will be resurrected just like Him. This truth allows me to grieve even now, but I grieve with hope. I know God is not finished yet.

www.ingramcontent.com/pod-product-compliance
Lightning Source LLC
LaVergne TN
LVHW010059110826
845155LV00028B/408

* 9 7 8 1 9 4 0 6 4 5 9 0 2 *